GOOD·OLD·DAYS
Country Wisdom™

Edited by Ken and Janice Tate

HOUSE of
WHITE
BIRCHES
PUBLISHERS
SINCE 1947

Country Wisdom™

Editors: Ken and Janice Tate
Managing Editor: Barb Sprunger
Copy Editors: Nicki Lehman, Mary Martin, Läna Schurb
Assistant Editors: Marla Freeman, Marj Morgan
Publication Coordinator: Tanya Turner

Production Coordinator: Brenda Gallmeyer
Graphic Arts Supervisor: Ronda Bechinski
Design/Production Artist: Erin Augsburger
Cover Design: Jessi Butler
Traffic Coordinator: Sandra Beres
Production Assistants: Janet Bowers, Chad Tate
Photography: Jeff Chilcote, Tammy Christian, Kelly Heydinger, Justin P. Wiard
Photography Assistant: Linda Quinlan

Publishers: Carl H. Muselman, Arthur K. Muselman
Chief Executive Officer: John Robinson
Marketing Director: Scott Moss
Book Marketing Manager: Craig Scott
Product Development Director: Vivian Rothe
Publishing Services Manager: Brenda Wendling

Customer Service: (800) 829-5865
Printed in the United States of America
First Printing: 2001
Library of Congress Number: 00-112313
ISBN: 1-882138-76-7

We would like to thank the following for the art prints used in this book:
Apple Creek Publishing: *Apple Spice* by Doug Knutson, pages 4 and 116. For information on art prints,
contact Apple Creek Publishing, Hiawatha, IA 52233, (800) 662-1707.

Mill Pond Press: *Passing Seasons* by Jim Daly, page 29; *Where Old Tires Go* by Jim Daly, page 52; *The Swing*
by Luke Buck, pages 56 and 57; *Home Remedy* by Jim Daly, pages 4 and 84; *Haying Time* by Jim Daly, pages 5 and 86;
A Month of Sundays by Jim Daly, pages 5, 98 and 99; *Hitching-Up* by Jim Daly, pages 3 and 110; *God's Country*
by Luke Buck, pages 132 and 133; *Holiday Treat* by Jim Daly, page 142; and *The Old Gang* by Jim Daly, pages 152 and 153.
For information on art prints, contact Mill Pond Press, Venice, FL 34292, (800) 535-0331.

Bob Pettes Nostalgic Impressions: *Cooper's Corner Store* by Bob Pettes, pages 4 and 12; and *After the Chores* by Bob Pettes,
pages 74 and 75. For information on art prints, contact Bob Pettes, Parkville, MO 64152, (816) 587-1754.

Wild Wings Inc.: *Golden Bounty-Canada Geese* by David Maass, pages 1 and 64; and *Creative Outlet* by Rollie Brandt,
pages 5 and 90. For information on art prints, contact Wild Wings Inc., Lake City, MN 55041, (800) 445-4833.

Dear Friends of the Good Old Days,

Our youngest daughter was the most adventurous of our children. From early in life she was the one who wanted to help with the cattle, hunt, fish and camp. Janice always said she had had her share of "roughing it" early in life, so if I wanted a partner for some adventure, Robin was usually elected to join me.

When she was a precocious 11-year-old, Robin and I went camping along the remote arm of a lake many miles down a gravel road in north Arkansas. Our campsite was not far from the old community of Enon and very close to where my great-grandfather Emmett Blevins lived, raised a family, died and was buried.

Grandpa Blevins, my Grandma Stamps' father, died three years before I was born, but while we were there I passed along stories passed to me by my mother, father and grandmother about Grandpa and life in the little community on that beautiful mountaintop.

I told her of my family's move to Oklahoma, followed by a move back to Arkansas after the death of my great-grandmother. I told her of the days when Daddy rode horseback to the little community for a dance at the little nondenominational church. We walked around the hillsides and I showed her the outlines of farmhouses, barns and sheds where once a thriving little village thrived, but where economics and drought had driven folks away many years before.

As we fished, I shared with her the secrets of angling my father shared with me and his father with him. The lake had covered my old fishing holes, but I told her of my own youthful adventures with Daddy and how they had shaped my life.

When Janice and I began putting together the heart and soul of this book, I thought back to that camping trip with Robin. How few today have the blessing of sharing the wisdom of one generation with the next! In the Good Old Days, fathers and mothers shared those bits of Country Wisdom with sons and daughters as the cycle of life turned from generation to generation.

Daddy taught me to crack a persimmon pit to forecast the harshness of the coming winter. If we found the interior of the pit to be shaped like a spoon, there would be lots of snow; if it was shaped like a fork, there would be little; if it was shaped like a knife, it would be bitterly cold. By the time my kids were older, such prognostication was viewed as nonsense, but I passed it along to my son, Chad, anyway.

This book is not just a compilation of snippets of Country Wisdom gleaned from the annals of the Good Old Days. Oh, yes, we have included those sayings, witticisms and truisms. But we have also included heartwarming stories of how that wisdom was put into practice, of how we learned the practical value of it all.

Just as Robin and I shared that special time together on that fishing trip when she was a youngster, we hope you will pull up a seat and "sit a spell." Laugh a little, cry a little and learn a lot as you experience these recollections of Country Wisdom from the Good Old Days.

Ken Tate

❧ Contents ❧

Healthful & Helpful Hints • 117

Proverbs & Superstitions • 143

Pennies Saved

Frugal. Thrifty. Economical. Those would be the words with which I would describe my upbringing. At times I might have even described it as parsimonious.

My maternal grandfather died when my mother was just a baby, initiating the Great Depression for that family long before the Great Depression was thought of by economists. Grandma Stamps never remarried, devoting her life to keeping home and hearth together for her three children.

My father was one of 14 children born to my Grandma and Grandpa Tate on their rocky farm in the Ozark Mountains. Just like Grandma Stamps, they had to constantly look for ways to make meals stretch a little farther. Ways to make worn out clothing last through just one more youngster. Ways to make the few dollars they had buy a few more necessities of life.

Mama and Daddy taught me through the example of their lives that "A penny saved is a penny earned." Sometimes saving a penny didn't mean you got to put it into a bank account. Most of the time it meant that the penny saved was spent on some other need, but at least we had it to spend. Reading the journal of expenses they kept through their early years of life together, it is easy to realize how saving pennies is what got them by.

Daddy kept the few pennies, nickels and dimes he could put back in the drawer of a bureau that set next to their bed. The farm didn't bring in many dollars in those days, so Daddy worked in a lumber mill in a nearby town to get our family by. He milked cows morning and evening; the milk money was the "gravy" on the meat and potatoes of our family budget.

Mama, like so many farm wives back in the Good Old Days, could have been a professional chef, a professional seamstress, a professional agronomist. She also proved herself as a pretty good economist. She took the money Daddy earned and treated it like it was made of rubber, as far as she stretched it.

My brother, sister and I couldn't think of our family as rich, but we never thought of ourselves as poor. It wasn't until I was an adult and could look back with a dispassionate eye to the home of my youth and realize it was little better than a shanty.

When I was a youngster, I learned early that if I wanted something that it would take some of Mama and Daddy's frugality to get it. They rarely had money to support a boy's sweet tooth or adventuresome spirit. If I wanted a bike, I needed to save the money to buy it myself. If I wanted to take in a movie, it was the same story. So after chores I ran errands for neighbors. Later I carried a paper route. There was always a way to earn a few cents and I saved those pennies until I could pay my own way.

Mama and Daddy's wise ways of saving pennies got Janice and me through some pretty tough times in the early years of our own marriage. Near the end of his life, Daddy told me he never worried whether I would be a good breadwinner. I smiled and said, "The nut doesn't fall far from the tree."

As I look over the stories in this chapter, I realize they echo the wisdom of Mama and Daddy, and their frugal, thrifty and, yes, parsimonious ways. They reflect how—through individual ingenuity, neighborly cooperation, hard work or just plain courtesy—pennies could be saved. Now that's Country Wisdom.

—Ken Tate

Surviving the Great Depression

By Donnie Kingman

"Use it up, wear it out, make it do, or do without." This was the way of life for my family during the Depression. My parents were dryland farmers in West Texas. In the midst of the Depression, they were hit with a devastating drought.

Many people were at the edge of hunger from 1929 until about 1935. The drought was widespread; the Depression was nationwide.

We were fortunate to live on a farm where we grew much of our food. We had cows for milk and chickens for meat and eggs. We had a garden, but it only grew when it rained.

We raised two black-and-white Hampshire pigs each year for meat. It was exciting when there was a little frost in the morning and the weather was cold enough so that we could butcher the pigs.

There's an old Southern expression about butchering that my grandmother used: "We'll save everything but the squeal." We made sausage and rendered the fat outside in a big, black, iron wash pot. My grandfather kept the fire going to render the fat. Then we had gallons of lard to store for another year. We hung the hams to cure, and salted the bacon down for the winter in the old meat box.

We did most of our socializing sitting around the big wooden table in a warm kitchen, sharing good food and interesting conversation with relatives and friends.

In the spring, after we had used all the meat, my mother cooked the meat skins with pinto beans or black-eyed peas. Sometimes she fried them in her old iron skillet and used the fat to make gravy. It tasted good over hot biscuits.

There didn't seem to be a recipe for her gravy. She just used any kind of fat; the best was drippings from the bacon, ham or sausage. She put the drippings in an old black skillet on the wood-burning stove. When it was hot, she added a handful of flour, a bit of salt and pepper, and poured in the liquid—milk, part milk and part water or, when there was no milk, just water. Water gravy was the last resort for many people. There is a saying: "Gravy saved more lives during the Depression than penicillin saves today."

Part of our food came from the wild game that lived in the canyon and on the hilly part of the farm. On cold, cloudy days, my father took the .22-caliber rifle and went hunting. Sometimes he brought back young rabbits and birds and prepared them for cooking. My mother cooked them on the old black wood-burning cookstove. We had fried rabbit or bird's breast and gravy.

If there wasn't enough to fry, she would make what she called Irish stew. She boiled the meat, and added onions, potatoes, salt and pepper. We ate it with corn bread made from homegrown, coarse-ground corn. We usually ate corn bread twice a day.

As the Depression worsened, so did the drought. It just wouldn't rain. The only time I remember seeing my mother desperate and seeming to lose hope was on a cold, dreary day in the old, drafty farmhouse that let sand and wind in around the windows and doors. We had no milk; the cows had gone dry. Mother was crying. She had used water, what cocoa she had, and some sugar to make us some hot chocolate.

Sometimes during the Depression we had food to share. We did most of our socializing sitting around the big wooden table in a warm kitchen, sharing good food and interesting conversation with relatives and friends.

My mother knew how to stretch the meat, beans or vegetables to make a good meal. She would stir up a plain cake for dessert. I remember the companionship and the fun we had more than the food.

The Dallas Semiweekly Farm News published pictures of men, women and children waiting in long soup lines with cups and pails. My mother and grandmother worried about so many people being hungry. We considered ourselves fortunate and were thankful to have food.

One Sunday we came home from church, hot and tired, in a wagon pulled by old Prince and Myrtle, our two big, red horses. (We had a Model-T, but no gas.) When we arrived and went inside, my mother said, "Someone has been here."

She went into the kitchen and saw that someone had taken the cold biscuits and beans. "Oh, well," she said, "someone must have been hungry."

She became upset, however, when she discovered that her little cut-glass bowl, a wedding present, was missing. It contained some special food, dried apricots. My grandfather ordered them from California and shared them with us. These were the first apricots we'd ever tasted. Later we found the bowl in the pasture where we kept the horses and cows; it was unbroken, with only a small chip on the bottom. Today the bowl is part of our family history.

Clothing also was a problem. We had no money for store-bought clothes. What clothes we had my mother sewed on her sewing machine. We received hand-me-downs and makeovers gratefully. School clothes were Mother's main concern, but she used any clothing given to her.

My mother used everything. She used the backs of worn-out overall legs to make pants for my brothers. The blue-and-white striped ones my grandfather gave her she made into overalls for the babies. My grandmother supplied flour and sugar sacks to make diapers and underwear. One of my favorite makeovers was a red coat and plaid skirt that my teacher, Mrs. Barker, gave my mother. I felt proud to wear it to church and school. My mother always wore the same old coat.

Sometimes my mother sold some old hens to buy us shoes, and they had to last all year. The year I was 9 years old, mine wore out in early spring and I had to go to school barefoot.

My brothers were glad to discard their worn, outgrown shoes as soon as the weather turned warm, but I found it humiliating. Later on, when the spring chickens were big enough to sell, my mother bought me some black patent leather Mary Jane shoes to wear to church.

The cotton crops provided a little money. We saved what we could for necessities and essential food such as flour, sugar, salt and coffee. In this way we survived the Depression.

We were never really hungry, although food was scarce at times.

We went to church and school and grew up with the values we learned during the Depression: to be thankful, to save, to share, and to have compassion for others. We learned to work hard and not to give up when things went bad. The example set by our parents and grandparents helped us survive and cope with life. ❖

Labor of Love

By Freda V. Fisher

It was a shock to come in from early morning chores to find my basket of ironing missing. Who would steal clean clothes and leave a radio and camera in the same room? I went from room to room, checking the entire house. Nothing else was missing. It was during the Depression. Perhaps someone had found the door open, saw the clothes, and hoped they would fit his family.

When the phone rang and my neighbor three miles away asked if I had missed anything that morning, I thought, Oh no! Hattie has been robbed, too! I soon found she was the robber instead.

She had come by, found the door open and no one home. She had taken the ironing to keep three lively teenage daughters busy and teach them housewife duties. It was summer vacation. She had six children and knew I would not likely let her take on more ironing.

It became a weekly routine to find my ironing missing if I was not in the house. It was a blessing for me, with two little ones and a farm to take care of while my husband worked at odd jobs to keep us afloat. Farm products were hard to sell when people had so little money.

Hattie refused to let me pay the girls. They also became free babysitters so we could attend night meetings or parties at the church. I finally managed to buy them some supplies in September when school began again. Hattie allowed them to accept the gifts. It was small pay for all their kind and generous service.

Hattie is gone now, and the girls are grown and married. I lost contact with them through the years. I am living far away in another state. I often wonder if someone did acts of kindness for them.

Maybe they will read this and know how grateful I am for their labor of love in those difficult but nostalgic days of the Depression. ❖

Old-Time Exchange

By Paul F. Long

*B*artering—exchanging one product for another without involving money—is as old as mankind. While little actual bartering may be done today, the terminology is still employed; often someone may talk about bartering for a car or some other item.

Bartering goods for goods or labor for goods or some other commodity was particularly important as a means of exchange when money was in short supply. For this reason, bartering has been especially prevalent during times of economic depression.

Early in American history, in remote little settlements on the frontier, barter was a common means of commercial transaction. Actually, the fact that these primitive establishments were called "trading posts" indicates the common means of exchange. Trading posts were a source of supplies and goods for Indians, trappers and settlers in the early period of American settlement.

Bartering was common from 1870 up into the 1940s, when locals often obtained groceries and household supplies by trading produce for them. Many older folks will remember bartering in little country stores. In fact, the language of that period recognized this; housewives commonly spoke of "doing their trading" at the grocery store on Saturday afternoon.

In the early days, three services in particular were often secured by barter. Gristmills generally were water-powered, and drew business to the settlement from customers many miles distant. If money was short—which was common in many households—part of the meal or grain was traded to the miller in payment for his services.

Sawmills were another frequent bartering site. Customers often traded timber to the sawmill in exchange for having lumber sawed.

A third place where bartering was used was the molasses or sugar mill. Sorghum cane stalks were hauled to these mills; in exchange for processing them into molasses or sugar, part of the product was given in exchange.

But for country people, the epitome of bartering was swapping horses. Horses and mules were the chief power source on the American farm until the latter 1930s, when trusty old Dobbins was put out to pasture by the gasoline tractor, especially the all-purpose machine that could be used for row crops.

For many individuals, purchasing or trading for draft animals for the farm went far beyond necessity. Just as their modern counterparts might have a passion for automobiles and delight in trading them, many persons in that earlier era took great pride in horse trading.

Horses might be swapped even up, or two or more for a single superior beast; in some cases, some money might be included to make up for the perceived difference in value.

The farmer who did not know horseflesh might fall victim to a more knowledgeable or unscrupulous trader. A "lemon" gotten in trade was likely swapped off as quickly as possible, perhaps in another community where its deficiencies were unknown. Perhaps the closest modern equivalent to horse trading would be dealing for a used car.

The Great Depression elevated bartering to a fine art. With money in short supply, both merchants and customers became highly creative. One type of barter which was especially common in rural communities was exchanging labor for labor, or labor for products. Hoboes who passed through communities frequently knocked at back doors to ask for food. They usually received a meal, often in exchange for splitting firewood or doing other chores.

One enterprising young salesman who was employed by the local implement dealer during the latter 1930s and early 1940s made a good thing out of bartering. The new gasoline-powered tractors offered many advantages over draft animals, so sales should have been brisk. Unfortunately, the emergence of the farm tractor coincided with the Depression, and money was scarce on the farm.

So the salesman accepted draft animals or other livestock as the down payment on a new farm tractor. While the allowance given for horses was not great, it did make a sale possible.

People also bartered for groceries. Nearly every farmer had laying hens and a herd of milk cows. On Saturday afternoon or Saturday night, when the grocery shopping was done, the eggs and cream were taken to town.

Often the grocer bought them and gave credit toward the purchase of groceries. Ideally, the credit for the produce was more than the grocery bill so a little cash was realized. For many farmers, especially in the Dust Bowl, the meager amount of money obtained from farm produce was the only real cash available.

Those old enough to remember will recall the peddlers who traveled through the countryside, stopping at farms to sell their goods to housewives. The McNess and Raleigh salesmen were the ones I vividly remember.

These itinerant salesmen brought not only delectable goodies and a great variety of nostrums, but also news and gossip of the outside world and our distant neighbors.

Often they would stay the night; they were welcome visitors in our insular lives.

In exchange for their goods, these peddlers often accepted poultry when money was not available. Salesmen selling subscriptions to such periodicals as Capper's Weekly and the Kansas City Star also accepted poultry in exchange.

I still recall one of these peddlers leaving our old farm with chickens in a crate—the payment—tied to the back of his buggy.

Another kind of Depression-era bartering occurred in a neighboring community, where the manager of the local theater used a creative approach to lure patrons when economic times were hard.

He placed this advertisement in a February 1933 issue of the local newspaper:

> *The Great Depression elevated bartering to a fine art. With money in short supply, both merchants and customers became highly creative.*

AT STATE THEATER

Will buy your wheat and produce!

Will exchange 10-cent and 25-cent show tickets for wheat, corn and eggs at the following prices.

*Eggs: 15 cents per dozen
*Yellow corn: at 30 cents per hundred
*White corn: at 27 cents per hundred
*Wheat: at 50 cents per bushel

Will accept any amount between 8 a.m. and 5 p.m. Tickets good at any show. Buyer at theater.

Today, in a period of relatively good times, plastic purchasing and easy credit, bartering is virtually unknown. We still may use some of the terminology—"making a trade," "swapping"—but the wise use of bartering has been largely relegated to the past, when times were hard and money was scarce. ❖

Neighbors

By Myra Baker

Editor's Note: Sometimes the wisdom of spending a few pennies paid off in longtime friendships in the farming communities of old. How much was it worth to have someone watching over you? That was what being neighbors was all about.—K.T.

They were farmers in a Midwestern community some 70 years ago or more— one, an older man nearing 70; the other, a younger man in his prime. The older man had more money than his younger neighbor, but not his physical strength.

In the spring there was always a young horse that needed to be broken. This was when farming was done with horses. The neighbors worked together to train a young horse to be a docile animal to pull the plow and cultivate the crops. The physical strength of the younger man was just what was needed to supplement the older man's understanding of animal nature.

Sudden torrential rains often came in the season of the hay harvest. The neighbors frequently laughed about the time the younger man had gone in the night to the attic of the older man's house and taken a canvas cover to save a half-formed stack of hay from being spoiled by the rain. The older man and his wife lay sound asleep while their attic was "robbed" of the canvas stack cover.

To save the straw for winter forage and bedding, someone had to stack the straw as it was blown from the separator of the threshing machine. The dust and chaff were unpleasant, especially when the stickers got inside your shirt. Stacking straw was a job the young man hated.

That winter, the younger man met his own difficulties. One of his children became seriously ill, and he lost several young hogs to cholera. When he couldn't afford to pay the premium on the health-and-accident policy he had carried for several years, he could do nothing but let it drop.

When, three months later, the notice came saying his premium was due again, the younger man noticed that the premium for the previous three months had been paid. He thought immediately of the older neighbor and approached him to thank him and to say he would repay him.

The older man's responded: "You saved my hay from the storm. You stacked my straw. Without your help, my colt would still be unbroken. What do I owe you?" ❖

Pinching Pennies

By Jack Chazen

Not that many years back, the chief economic adviser to the president issued a statement saying that because of the severe shortage of pennies, the gross national product would decline sharply. And if nothing would be done about it, merchants would be forced to round off all sales to the nearest nickel, which in turn would cause a surge in inflation.

But here's the simple truth of the matter: If this big economic adviser would visit his mother once in a while, he'd know why we're short of pennies. Everybody and his grandmother filled up coffee cans and cookie jars with them, saving for "rainy days," or just hoping to get a little ahead of the wolf that seemed to be constantly at the door.

When I was a kid, a penny was a medium of exchange, not a medium for change. In those days, people squeezed everything they could out of a penny, but at least there was something to squeeze.

Today people look at a penny with contempt—drop one and see if anybody will pick it up. Even my grandson won't. But I don't blame him, because I know for a fact that he has a rich grandfather. Still, if he continues in this vein, he may someday be chief economic advisor to the president.

Years ago you could actually spend a penny. There were penny postcards, penny arcades and penny bubblegum machines. Immies were a penny, and Con Edison used to advertise, "Look at all the electricity a penny will buy." Of course, we also had 2-cent stamps and 2-cent chocolate bars. We even had the Two-Penny Opera, and if you were rich, a nickel would get you a charlotte russe.

The biggest bargain was a newspaper. For 2 cents you read it, wrap a herring in it, and it was useful in the facility out the door and down the path.

As kids, we used to sing, "Shave and a haircut, two bits." Nowadays a haircut is more like 80 bits or more. Doesn't sound right, does it? And how many bits do you need for a shoeshine? That is, if you could find a bootblack. Nowadays, I keep a roll of quarters on hand just in case my grandson wants to indulge himself in one of those video arcade machines.

I guess I liked the Good Old Days because I didn't have to think in terms of paper money. Wooden nickels I understood; trolley-car transfers I understood, and cigar-store coupons I understood.

When I heard the economic advisers say that the national debt had reached $2 trillion, I couldn't even remember if a trillion had six or nine zeros. I ran to the dictionary. Under "T" I found trillion defined as a thousand billion, written as a 1 with 12 zeros. That would be 1,000,000,000,000 right? I wonder how much electricity that would buy!

If you were lucky enough to have a job back in the Good Old Days, you would line up 10 cents in the morning. For that you got three cigarettes, the Daily News and a subway ride. For lunch, a dime would get you a bowl of soup and two rolls—with butter, yet. And 10 cents would get you into the movie where the latest episode of *The Perils of Pauline* was sandwiched between two first-run pictures, the *Pathé News* and a Betty Boop cartoon.

The way we used pennies back then, it's no wonder there has been the threat of a penny shortage. Whether we were pinching them, saving them or exchanging them, we sure understood the value of the little copper coin. ❖

Where the Buffalo Roamed

By Carl W. Maiwald

The Chinese have the Year of the Dragon, the Year of the Monkey, the Year of the Rat, etc.—but 1913 was "the Year of the Buffalo" in the United States. They appeared by the hundreds of thousands and were as welcome as lemonade on a dog day afternoon. Their numbers increased annually until just about everyone and his sister had at least a few.

You don't see these beasts around nowadays, but there are still a few choice specimens in the hands of folks who like having them tucked away in various cubbyholes, or on display.

Life was more tranquil back then. The horseless carriage had not yet driven out Ol' Dobbin and we had no Air Force because "flying machines" were considered "crazy contraptions" whose sole purpose was to frighten chickens so they quit laying. Clergymen would call down the wrath of God on aviators, vowing, "Only fools and feathers fly."

But 1913's halcyon days were not fated to last much longer; it was a year of change. Richard M. Nixon arrived on the scene, as did yours truly C.W. Maiwald, the first income tax and the buffalo nickel. The buffalo nickel was so popular because nickels were probably the most useful coin of that era when electricity and gaslights were struggling for supremacy.

Much could be bought with that "jitney." You could get two first-class stamps plus a penny postcard for your nickel. A quart of milk, a loaf of bread or a pint of lager cost the same.

Your jit would also get you a subway ride, taxi service or a fat, succulent hot dog on a roll with all the trimmings. It was also the coin most likely to land in the collection plate at church.

And don't forget the double-dip ice-cream cones, bag of candy, movie matinees and sarsaparilla soda pop for us kids!

The nickel was a proper tip for a waitress, and what you paid a kid to shovel your walk or run an errand. Last but not least, the jit would buy the Sunday newspaper with the comics: *The Katzenjammer Kids, Foxy Grandpa,* and *Mutt and Jeff.*

Shrewd old Frank W. Woolworth became a multimillionaire with his five-and-ten–cent stores. Now, these paltry coins are just chicken feed that wouldn't pay the state sales tax on most purchases.

We will never see the return of the buffalo. ❖

> *The buffalo nickel was so popular because nickels were probably the most useful coin of that era when electricity and gaslights were struggling for supremacy.*

Pennies Saved, Pennies Paid

Editor's Note: *For many years I have said that there was more wisdom in the empty pocket of a farmer than in the full coffers of a bureaucrat. Perhaps nations would be better off if the treasuries were managed by the frugality of a farm wife.*

In 1913, the majority of Americans lived "down on the farm." Farm income then, as today, was not very high, but if you had a bit of money it went a long way.

Now if you're like me, every year when you prepare your taxes, you wish that it could be a lot simpler. The Almighty just asks for a flat 10 percent; isn't there some way it could be that simple with the government?

Well, looking back to the way income taxes was computed in 1913, perhaps we would be better off to return to those simpler times. I ran across the tax form for that year and was amused and amazed by its simple, 20-point plan. Here are all the instructions provided in those days in the early part of the 20th century.

—K.T.

1. This return shall be made by every citizen of the United States, whether residing at home or abroad, and by every person residing in the United States, though not a citizen thereof, having a net income of $3,000 or over for the taxable year and also by every nonresident alien deriving income from property owned and business, trade or profession carried on in the United States by him.

2. When an individual by reason of minority, sickness or other disability, or absence from the United States is unable to make his own return, it may be made for him by his duly authorized representative.

3. The normal tax of 1 percent shall be assessed on the total net income less the specific exemption of $3,000 or $4,000 as the case may be. (For the year 1913, the specific exemption allowable is $2,500, or $3,333.33, as the case may be.) If,

however, the normal tax has been deducted and withheld on any part of the income at the source, or if any part of the income is received as dividends upon the stock or from the net earnings of any corporation, etc., which is taxable upon its net income, such income shall be deducted from the individual's total net income for the purpose of calculating the amount of income on which the individual is liable for the normal tax of 1 percent by virtue of this return.

4. The addition or super tax shall be calculated as stated on page 1.

5. This return shall be filed with the Collector of Internal Revenue for the district in which the individual resides if he has no other place of business; otherwise, in the district in which he has his principal place of business; or in case the person resides in a foreign country, then with the collector for the district in which his principal business is carried on in the United States.

6. This return must be filed on or before the first day of March succeeding the close of the calendar year for which the return is made.

7. The penalty for failure to file the return within the time specified by law is $20 to $1,000. In case of refusal or neglect to render the return within the required time (except in cases of sickness or absence), 50 percent shall be added to amount of tax assessed. In case of false or fraudulent return, 100 percent shall be added to such tax, and any person required by law to make, render, sign, or verify any return who makes any false or fraudulent return or statement with intent to defeat or evade the assessment required by this section to be made shall be guilty of a misdemeanor, and shall be fined not exceeding $2,000 or be imprisoned not exceeding one year, or both, at the discretion of the court, with the costs of prosecution.

8. When the return is not filed within the required time by reason of sickness or absence

of the individual, an extension of time, not exceeding 30 days from March 1, within which to file such return, may be granted by the collector, provided an application therefore is made by the individual within the period for which such extension is desired.

9. This return properly filled out must be made under oath or affirmation. Affidavits may be made before any officer authorized by law to administer oaths. If before a justice of the peace or magistrate not using a seal, a certificate of the clerk of the court as to the authority of such officer to administer oaths should be attached to the return.

10. Expenses for medical attendance, store accounts, family supplies, wages of domestic servants, cost of board, room or house rent for family or personal use, are not expenses that can be deducted from gross income. In case an individual owns his own residence he cannot deduct the estimated value of his rent, neither shall he be required to include such estimated rental of his home as income.

11. The farmer, in computing the net income from his farm for his annual return, shall include all moneys received for produce and animals sold, and for the wools and hides of animals slaughtered, provided such wool and hides are sold, and he shall deduct therefrom the sums actually paid as purchase money for the animals sold or slaughtered during the year.

12. In calculating losses, only such losses as shall have been actually sustained and the amount of which has been definitely ascertained during the year covered by the return can be deducted.

13. Persons receiving fees or emoluments for professional or other services, as in the case of physicians or lawyers, should include all actual receipts for services rendered in the year for which return is made, together with all unpaid accounts, charges for services, or contingent income due for that year, if good and collectible.

14. Debts which were contracted during the year for which return is made, but found in said year to be worthless, may be deducted from gross income for said year, but such debts cannot be regarded as worthless until after legal proceedings to recover the same have proved fruitless, or it clearly appears that the debtor is insolvent. If debts contracted prior to the year for which return is made were included as income in return for year in which said debts were contracted, and such debts shall subsequently prove to be worthless, they may be deducted under the head of losses in the return for the year in which such debts were charged off as worthless.

15. Amounts due or accrued to the individual members of a partnership from the net earnings of the partnership, whether apportioned and distributed or not, shall be included in the annual return of the individual.

16. United States pensions shall be included as income.

17. Estimated advance in value of real estate is not required to be reported as income, unless the increased value is taken up on the books of the individual as an increase of assets.

18. Costs of suits and other legal proceedings arising from ordinary business may be treated as an expense of such business, and may be deducted from gross income for the year in which such costs were paid.

19. An unmarried individual or a married individual not living with wife or husband shall be allowed an exemption of $3,000. When husband and wife live together they shall be allowed jointly a total exemption of only $4,000. They may make a joint return, both subscribing thereto, or if they have separate incomes, they may make separate returns; but in no case shall they jointly claim more than $4,000 exemption on their aggregate income.

20. In computing net income there shall be excluded the compensation of all officers and employees of a State or any political subdivision thereof, except when such compensation is paid by the United States Government. ❖

Depression Cost of Living

By Leona E. Chestnut

Remember when it cost $3.50 to get a marriage license? That's what it cost my sweetheart to make our marriage legal in 1932. Seems odd, too. More of us stayed married when the fee was minimal than folks do today. We didn't go to Niagara Falls for our honeymoon. We were content to drive 20 miles to a romantic old hotel that had once been a gristmill. We watched the water run over the dam and dreamed our dreams of the future.

I remember when the doctor came to our house to deliver our first baby. He charged $20. What kind of a baby can you get for $20 today?

We were farmers. My husband worked for the more affluent farmers for $1 a day. But then, it evened out; he could buy a pair of denim overalls for 98 cents. That was in 1933, B.S.T. (before sales tax).

I taught the District 7 School and received $70 a month. We thought that was a fine salary. Our money went farther in those days. We could buy a 50-pound sack of flour for 89 cents and a 10-pound sack of sugar for 49 cents. We could buy *Grit* magazine for a nickel and *The Saturday Evening Post* for a dime.

We lived through the Depression, Kansas dust storms, droughts, hail storms and the grasshopper plague, and we didn't go on Relief. When an occasional vagrant stopped for a meal, we gave him scrambled eggs, stewed tomatoes with bread and butter—the same food we ate.

That was before the days of rural electrification in our area. We used kerosene lamps and sadirons, and washed our clothes in a tub on a washboard. We didn't even have an icebox. To keep butter and milk cool we put them in a bucket and hung the bucket down the well.

We milked one cow and set the milk overnight for the cream to rise. In the morning we skimmed the cream off, sold it, and drank the skim milk.

The first year of our marriage we bought an incubator. We set 150 eggs in it and in three weeks, we had 120 little chickens. When the chickens were about 6 weeks old, a storm came along and blew away the brooder house, but left the chickens. We went out in the pouring rain, slogged through the mud and, soaked to the skin, collected the chickens. (Wet chickens stink!)

We brought the waterlogged chicks into the kitchen, dried them off and put them in the oven of the wood-burning range to warm up.

We bought chicken feed that came in beautifully colored print material. When the sack was empty I washed it and used it to make aprons, curtains, or a little girl's dress. Many farm wives bought the feed two or three sacks at a time, and chose sacks with the same print pattern. Three sacks were enough to make a housedress. They wore them to church, too.

We had a Model-T Ford that was prone to have flat tires. It could speed down the road (on the level) at 40 mph. It went downhill faster. But we could fill old Lizzie's gas tank for about a dollar.

The first year we farmed, we had no tractor or horse. To plow our garden, we borrowed a horse from a neighbor. When the potatoes and sweet corn needed to be cultivated, my husband hitched the horse to a single-row cultivator. I had to lead the horse because he had a penchant for walking on the corn instead of between the rows. The beast just seemed to delight in putting his 10-inch foot on every other stalk of corn. He didn't mind putting his foot on me, either.

Country folks had the wisdom to manage things back then. Can't say I'd like to live again in those Good Old Days, but they certainly weren't bad, either. ❖

For Dogs Only

By Sheila Julson

Editor's Note: *Many times the pennies we spend today on simple things were saved back in the Good Old Days using the simple wisdom of making it for ourselves.—K.T.*

I walked over to my grandmother's house one spring afternoon. As I rounded the corner by the kitchen, a slight aroma tipped me off to the fact that Grandma had been baking. When I entered the kitchen, little round biscuits were cooling on a rack.

"Hi, Grandma," I said reaching for a biscuit.

"You put that down," she warned. "They're for the dog."

"For the dog!" I echoed, as I put the biscuit back on the rack. I pondered over that, for making homemade treats for our four-legged pals was something I had never seen.

Grandma, reading my mind, explained how and why she made dog biscuits.

When she was a child during the Great Depression with five brothers and sisters, money was tight for her family. Her brothers and sisters wanted to take in a neighborhood stray dog, but her mother was set against it.

"No," she would tell my grandmother, "we can barely afford to feed us, let alone neighborhood animals."

However, Grandma adored the stray dog and was not thwarted by my great-grandmother's response. When her father was out doing odd side jobs, and while her mother took a break from baking bread to chat with a neighbor, the children raided the icebox.

It was then that their mother informed them that they had fed that night's supper to a dog.

They wrapped up leftover sausages in a flour-sack towel and proceeded to the back alley where the stray was likely to be found. The dog ate all of the sausages ravenously.

After playing with the dog for a while, my grandma and her brothers and sisters went home. It was then that their mother informed them that they had fed that night's supper to a dog.

Puzzled about how she knew they had taken the sausages, and why she was so angry, the children cried. Taking pity on them, their mother concocted a snack for the dog to prevent anything like that from happening again.

She was already baking bread, so all the supplies were out. She sparingly mixed basic bread ingredients and added flavoring so it was just the right snack for a dog. It only cost pennies to make, unlike the boxed dog biscuits from the market.

"Well, that was a good idea," I told Grandma after she explained the story.

"Yes," she said, "and it's healthier for dogs, too. The oil gives them a shiny coat, and these biscuits are better for them. They don't have all that junk in them like store-bought biscuits do."

"How do you remember how she made them?" I asked.

"It's one of those things that you just know," she said, smiling. "I altered them a bit over the years, but they're about the same as when your great-grandma made them. The dog liked them, and we never took food from the icebox again."

I was about to put the biscuits to the true test. I tossed one down on the floor for Sassy, Grandma's dachshund. He gobbled it up and flashed his sad, brown eyes at me—his "beggar's look"—pleading for another biscuit.

"Yep," I told Grandma, "these biscuits are pretty good." ❖

Grandma's Dog Biscuits

6 tablespoons oil

1 egg

1/2 cup milk

1/4 cup water

2 1/2 cups wheat flour

Pinch of minced onion or garlic

1/2 teaspoon salt

Beef, bacon, or chicken fat for flavor (Grandma also used beef or chicken bouillon cubes.)

Preheat oven to 350 degrees. Mix liquids first, then add flour and other ingredients.

The mixture will have the consistency of bread dough. Roll 1/2-inch thick on floured board and cut into shapes.

Place on greased cookie sheet and bake for 35–40 minutes.

When a Dime Was a Dime

By Barbara Weber

Editor's Note: *It used to be that people had respect for this little coin. Remember when a dime bought more than 10 pennies?—K.T.*

while back, Ann Landers wrote something that really made me stop and think, or rather stop and remember. She wrote: "It used to be an allowance and now it's an emergency screwdriver ..." What was she talking about? A dime.

Remember those?

A lot of people today don't even bend over to pick one up anymore, but, ah, the dimes of my life!

Remember when a dime bought more than 10 pennies? Remember when it actually bought a couple of stamps and two packages of gum? Now it's just a down payment!

And remember when a dime bought an ice-cream bar or a bottle of RC Cola? Gee, do they still make RC Cola? Do they even put soda in glass bottles anymore?

And a phone call? Remember how you could use a pay phone for only a dime? And how scandalized everybody was when it went from a nickel to a dime?

I think what I remember most about dimes, though, is going to the movies with Uncle Edgar. He was my mother's uncle—a forbidding sort of man who wore those little glasses without any rims. My mother said he owned a small "loan company." My father said it was a pawnshop.

Uncle Edgar would come to visit us once in awhile, and for some reason, he always felt obliged to take me to a movie. I didn't particularly like going with him because, well, let's face it, it's hard to enjoy a show with someone who always looks like his shoes are too tight. But a movie was a movie.

But when it came to buying candy he was the worst! I remember him solemnly laying a dime on the candy counter and buying a single bag of plain M&Ms. Then, throughout the entire movie, he grimly doled them out to me, one at a time. After all, this was a dime's worth of candy. In his mind that should be more than enough for two people for an entire movie.

There were times, mighty seldom as I recall, when he was in an expansive mood and would buy 5-cents' worth of candy for me and a Mounds bar for himself. Wow! A Mounds bar!

"Mounds bars," he explained gravely, "are not for children. They are only for adults; they cost a dime." It was as if the pope had spoken.

Needless to say, I never brought up that subject again. And, you know? To this day I still look on Mounds bars, or any other "adult" candy bars that at one time had cost "a whole dime," with a kind of awe. This was because back then, as Uncle Edgar explained, a dime was a dime, not an emergency screwdriver. ❖

Country Courtesy Has Its Rewards

By Bob Plack

I remember the day well, because I was sitting in the front seat of our Reo Silver Power panel truck, rattling down the country road. (I seldom enjoyed the luxury of sitting in the front seat. That was Mom's place. My sister and I normally sat on apple boxes in the back.)

My joy was short-lived, though, 'cause Dad ordered me to the apple box when he saw the man walking ahead of us. (Dad never passed anyone on a deserted road without offering a ride.) So before we even stopped, I disliked this stranger.

He shuffled along, dust billowing up to his knees and a bridle tossed over his shoulder. A sweat-stained straw hat and worn bib overalls identified him as a farmer. We weren't sure where he was going, but the closest house was at least two miles away.

Dad stopped the truck. "Lose your horse, mister?" The man turned to face the cloud of dust surrounding us. Dad opened the door and said, "Hop in."

He was older than he looked from a distance. We later learned that he was 80. He tugged and pulled, finally mounting the high running board step, then settled into the seat.

Seventeen acres must be almost the whole world. Maybe I could have a dog, and raise rabbits in the shed, and float boats in the spring, and catch frogs!

"How far you goin'?" Dad asked.

"'Bout three miles."

"That's a pretty long walk. What happened to your horse?"

"Rode him to the pasture."

Silence followed as Dad nursed the Reo up to speed. The carburetor needed adjusting and the fuel pump sometimes needed whacking, so we were

lucky to go at all. The old man stared straight ahead, resisting all attempts at conversation.

"This sure is pretty countryside," Dad said. "Do you know of a small farm with a house that might be for sale?"

That just about tipped over my apple box. I'd never heard Dad talking about buying a house, especially in the country. I couldn't wait to tell Sis. She hated living in back of the deserted Frankie and Johnny Restaurant even more than I did. She even had to sleep with Mom and Dad at night because she was scared of the scurrying noises on the floor.

He looked at Dad and said, "I'll sell you 17 acres with a two-room house and 'lectricity. The well's good and the outhouse is new. And there's a couple of sheds and a spring that runs year-round."

I pictured paradise. Seventeen acres must be almost the whole world. Maybe I could have a dog, and raise rabbits in the shed, and float boats in the spring, and catch frogs! I'd trade playin' in the dusty alley behind the restaurant for a farm any day. It'd be even better than my uncle's farm, 'cause we'd live there.

"Sounds good to me," Dad said. "How much you askin'?"

"Forty-five hundred dollars."

That figured. Forty-five hundred dollars must be more money than in the whole world. We didn't have enough to get the car fixed. Now I really hated this guy.

Dad didn't have anything to say after that. The man motioned to pull over near a long,

tree-lined lane and said, "I don't need the money all at once. Fifty dollars down and 10 payments over 10 years at 2 percent interest, and it's yours."

"Well, it sounds OK, but I don't have $50."

The old man lowered himself to the ground and stared at Dad. The frozen scene became uncomfortable and the old man broke the silence. "Thanks for the ride."

"You're welcome."

Dad began to coax the Reo into action when we heard yelling through the sputtering engine noise. "Hold on!" The door opened. "How 'bout if I loan you $50 and you pay it back the first year?'

I thought this guy must be as rich as anybody. Dad said, "Mister, if I like the place, you got a deal."

He arranged to see the property two days later and the deal went through. Within a week we moved in.

The years passed and I got a dog, caught frogs, raised rabbits and helped farm. The old man, J.W., was a good neighbor and we traded farm work. He hired me part time sometimes, but always paid Dad for my work because I was a minor. I didn't mind though. Dad always gave me my due and J.W. let me drive his new Farmall Cub tractor.

Driving that tractor rated second only to riding in the passenger seat of the Reo, and no longer did J.W. have to ride the plowhorse to pasture or walk home up the dusty road with the bridle over his shoulder. Lucky for us though, J.W. didn't have a tractor the day we drove up that road back in 1941. ❖

Patches of the Past

By Kathryn Nutt

One of the most important lessons I learned from my parents and grandparents was the wisdom of knowing how to make a good patch. By definition, a patch is a piece of material used to mend or cover something. Different kinds of patches were very important to me through my life.

As a nurse, I take care of many elderly people. One of my patients commented to me, "Just call me 'Patches.' I'm falling apart." We both laughed. When I took off her stockings to cut her toenails, she had little square bandages covering areas of broken skin, corn pads and a pad over her bunion. Her feet did look like they had patches on them.

I'm fondly reminded of our springer spaniel named Patches. Patches had black ears and black over her eyes, covering both halves of her face, with a white stripe down the center. She had a big, black patch on the middle of her back and a smaller one at the base of her tail. The rest of her body was white with an underlining of little black freckles. She loved to play in the water and always was good for a swim or two in the river when we went fishing. She was a great companion.

I also remember the quilt patches my grandmother and mother used to make beautiful quilts. It was always fun to pick out the pieces of material that were scraps of my dresses or Grandma's apron or pot holders.

The quilt patches were cut in several shapes according to what quilt Grandma was making. But

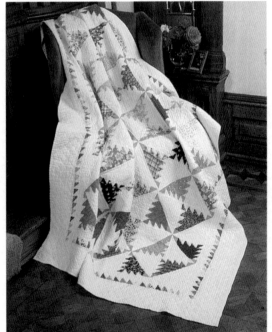

no matter what their shape, when all the patches were put together, the quilts were beautiful.

As my son was growing up, I put patches on his jeans. The knees always wore out first. I patched the girls' jeans, too, and cut different shapes, like kittens, flowers or cars, so they would think they were cute rather than mended.

Grandma used to mend the heels of socks with a patch from another sock. She also mended sheets that wore thin in the middle with a patch from another sheet that had some good left on the edges. Patches have made many clothes and linens wear a little longer in times when money was very short.

Grandma used to laugh about an apron that just covered her dress below the waist. She called the half-apron a "belly-patch apron." To this day, when I tie on an apron, I think of Grandma.

Remember the patches that held that old tire together? Tire patches are much better now than back when the old Model-T tires needed one patch after another.

Remember the patch that Long John Silver wore over his eye in *Treasure Island*? "That was a scary sight, Matey!" With the new technology, he probably would have just had a glass eye put in and we would never have experienced the character of Long John Silver.

Whether decorating a person as healing bandages, the spots of a pet, or creating a beautiful patchwork quilt, patches were a wonderful way to hold things together back in the Good Old Days. ❖

The Kindest Man I Ever Met

By Nelson J. Lauth

*I*n May 1944, we moved into our house near Kenmore, N.Y. That first day was a hectic one, moving in and getting settled, but it was a happy day, for we had spent five years in rent, scraping together the down payment for our new home.

As we were arranging the furniture in a rear bedroom, we chanced to look out the window. There, in our backyard, was a man we had never seen before. He was kneeling, intently putting something in the ground. When we went out to investigate, he introduced himself.

"I am George McKernan, your next-door neighbor," he said. "I'm giving you a start with your garden. These are multiplier onions. If you'll pinch off the little onion sets that grow on the top of the stems, and press them into the ground, you will never want for cooking onions."

We were surprised by this unexpected act of kindness. We thanked him and invited him into the house for coffee and doughnuts. He readily accepted.

As we sat across the table from him that first morning, talking, we were filled with the warmth this gentle, soft-spoken man conveyed to us.

Mr. McKernan was in his mid-60s. He had recently retired as an English teacher at our local high school. He was obviously of Irish extraction. His full, pink, puckish face became animated and there was a twinkle in his eyes as he talked. He and his wife were married for nearly 40 years. They had one son, Brian, who was grown and married. Brian worked for the post office, and had a supervisory position in Boulder, Colo. He and his wife came back to Kenmore once a year at Christmastime to visit.

Mr. McKernan had a genuine love for gardening. His backyard, though small, was beautifully laid out with a luxuriant array of flowers on one side and neat rows of vegetables on the other, with a carefully laid flagstone walk down the middle. It put my yard, with its great clumps of crabgrass, weeds and bare spots, to shame, but I had neither the time nor inclination to tackle another job.

> *One day I offered George a can of his favorite pipe tobacco. He seemed quite embarrassed. It was only after much coaxing that he accepted it, but somehow, I felt I had done him an injustice.*

Several days after his first visit, we were in for our second surprise. I answered a knock at our door one evening. There was Mr. McKernan with a rather sheepish look on his face. He had a sheet of paper in his hand.

"I have something here I would like to show you if you have the time," he said simply.

"Of course," I answered. "Come right in."

We sat down in the living room. On a sheet of paper was a neat sketch of our backyard. With enthusiasm, he exclaimed, "All you'd have to do, Mr. Lauth, is buy the vegetable seed you want. Our flowerbed needs thinning out. There's enough flowers for both our yards. I can do the job in no time at all. What do you say?" With that question, his voice took on a pleading tone.

I was astounded! Here was a man almost begging me to undertake a task that involved a good deal of work. For a moment I was silent. Finally, "Mr. McKernan, your offer is a most generous one, but I could not allow you to do all that work without some compensation. We should agree on some ..."

"Mr. Lauth," he broke in, with a stern look on his face I hadn't seen before, "I would be obliged if we never mention pay again; pay is for strangers. We are friends!"

Hastily, I started to blurt out an apology, but thought better of it. "OK, if you must have it that way. I would never dispute our friendship."

"Another thing," he said. "I don't think there should be any 'Misters'; just call me George."

I wished I had thought to say that. From that time on, we were just common everyday George and Nelson.

Often, I would come home from work expecting to cut the front lawn to find that George's power mower had been there first. "Need the exercise," he would say simply.

One morning as we sat down to breakfast, our old electric toaster refused to work. We had another one, so I threw the old one on top of the garbage can in back of the house. That evening, back from work, I found it by the side door with a note. "Just a loose connection in the cord plug," the note said. No signature.

A picket I had knocked off the fence one morning as I was backing the car out of the yard was neatly replaced when I arrived home that evening.

I answered a knock at our door one evening. There was Mr. McKernan with a rather sheepish look on his face. He had a sheet of paper in his hand.

One day I offered George a can of his favorite pipe tobacco. He seemed quite embarrassed. It was only after much coaxing that he accepted it, but somehow, I felt I had done him an injustice. After that, when we picked up something we thought he would be pleased with, we gave it to his wife to give to him. We knew, of course, that he was aware of where these little gifts came from. Though he never mentioned them or thanked us directly, we sensed he was pleased, for immediately after one of these incidents, we were surprised by an unexpected favor. The puddles in the middle of our garage floor, caused by a leaky roof, suddenly disappeared; the wild wisteria that grew on an arbor bordering our yards was carefully tacked and trimmed; a beautiful little magnolia tree appeared like magic on our front lawn.

There was a time when I didn't see George for a week, but each evening, I could see our barren yard being transformed into a beautiful garden. When he finished the job, he brushed away our enthusiastic praise. "If there's something you don't like, let me know," he said,

and walked away.

Then, suddenly, after a brief illness, Mrs. McKernan died. My wife and I were shocked at the abruptness of her death. Brian and his wife flew in from Boulder late that evening.

I spent a big part of the next two days at the funeral parlor, helping where I could. We attended the funeral. After it was over, we invited the three of them over to our house, but George quietly declined.

Brian and his wife stayed for three more days and then returned to Colorado. After they had gone, we invited George over to the house for dinner. Again, he declined. It was clear that he wished to be alone in his grief.

Several weeks later, I chanced upon him in his backyard. I called him over to the fence. The twinkle had gone from his eyes. His face had taken on a gray pallor.

"George, why not sell the house and live with us? The spare bedroom is yours. You are family to us. We'd be happy if you would."

He put his hand on my arm and pressed it hard, shaking his head slowly. "No," he said quietly. "Don't think I don't appreciate your kind offer. …" His voice drifted away. Then he continued, "My son and daughter-in-law have asked me to come out to Colorado for a while." His face brightened. "I have a new grand-daughter, you know. Brian phoned last night." He took my hand and pressed it in his. "God willing, we will meet again. Sometimes goodbyes are better left unsaid." With that he turned and went into the house.

Two days later, early in the morning, George backed his car out of the driveway. We never saw him again. A month later, we received a letter from Brian. George had passed away in his sleep.

A great void has come into our lives since that day. But we still have an ample supply of multiplier onions—a good deed that has lasted all these years—and our vivid memories of George McKernan, the kindest man I ever met. ❖

John
Slobodnik

Common Sense

❧

*I*t seems that common sense is very uncommon in today's world. Whatever became of the grassroots wisdom that seemed to emanate from the heartland back in the Good Old Days?

Those of us who were blessed to be raised out in the country picked up much of our common sense from the common sayings of the times. It was no coincidence that our most common of sayings were directly tied to life on the farm.

I still have a tendency, when making an appointment, to depart with the condition that I will see them "if the good Lord's willing and the creeks don't rise." This combination of the physical and spiritual was probably my earliest introduction to the workings of God. It was Grandma's way of saying that she never knew for sure what the morrow might bring.

But it was a lot more than just a biblical enjoinder to that country woman. In her 91 years of life she never drove anything but a horse and buggy, and most of her travel was by "shank's mare"— in other words, on foot. That meant crossing many a creek and stream in the hilly Ozark Mountains where we lived. If a rain pushed up the creek and flooded the fords, it mattered little if the good Lord was willing. Grandma wouldn't make it across and the visit would have to be canceled.

Proverbs about animals taught me and my country kith and kin a lot about life. After working or riding a horse or mule for awhile, we knew the animal should be cooled down, stalled, watered and fed. Daddy once told me that our plow horse Dandy looked like he had been "rode hard and put away wet." Later the phrase was applied to a neighbor who had had a tough day in the fields. I came to understand the connection between taking care of our animals and taking care of ourselves.

"What's good for the goose is good for the gander." That was Mama's way of putting Daddy in his place if she thought he was treating her unfairly in some way. Janice had the same kind of upbringing, so I have had several "goose and gander" moments in our decades of marriage.

One of my favorite sayings from my youth is, "That dog won't hunt." When I was a youngster, we used dogs to track, tree and hunt everything from deer to coons to squirrels. If a dog just wouldn't tree a coon or squirrel, we just said, "That dog won't hunt," and got rid of him as soon as possible. When I say that, what I mean is, "That's not a good enough excuse or explanation." I remember when my son came in past curfew one time with the lamest of excuses. I looked him square in the eyes and intoned, "That dog won't hunt!" When Papa used that phrase, a wise son knew never to let it happen again. He didn't.

When life dealt us a cruel twist of fate—like the time fire razed two of our crucial hay stacks counted on for winter grazing, Daddy said, "Let's not cry over spilt milk." For any country boy or girl who has squeezed out a pail of milk from an ornery old Jersey or Guernsey just to have her put a hoof right into the bucket, spilling every drop, this truism means a lot. There is no reason to agonize over that which we simply have no control.

"The fiddler calls the tune" was another proverb I was able to understand from life around the farm. Whether it was a hoe-down or just one of our family music parties, those who played the tunes determined what tunes would be played. From the old saying I came to understand that you have to work hard if you want to be in the position to make the decisions. I never learned to play the fiddle, but I developed some common sense from the proverb.

These stories and compilations of wit and wisdom from these proverbs and sayings will help you remember the common sense we had back in those uncommon times called the Good Old Days.

—Ken Tate

They Used to Say ...

By Patricia Keller

O nce upon a time, in a slower, less hectic time—back when our parents were just youngsters and our grandparents were not yet grandparents—people had a slightly different way of expressing themselves.

Their brief phrases conveyed a weighty message, giving advice, offering warnings or just making a statement on life in general.

Times have changed, and today life is lived at a pace that would have been unthinkable then, but those sayings are just as true and as applicable today as they were then. Many of those sayings are true gems of wisdom. We can benefit from their insights and we can chuckle at some of the unusual ways of commenting about life in an honest, more direct way.

The sayings often dealt with work, its relationship to people and people's relationship to it. They used to say:

"Idle hands are the devil's tools."

"Many hands make light work."

"There's learning in doing."

"Busy people don't have time to be busybodies."

"If you aim at nothing, that is what you're sure to hit."

"The person who never makes a mistake is the person who never does anything."

Sometimes they referred to strategies for getting along with others, methods for handling life's situations. They used to say:

"You can catch more flies with honey than you can with vinegar."

"The secret of happiness is not found in doing what you like, but in liking what you do."

"Don't trouble trouble 'til trouble troubles you."

"Actions speak louder than words."

"It's better to sleep on what you intend to do than to stay awake over what you have done."

Sometimes their words were simply gems of wisdom to help us see life realistically and to live it fully. They used to say:

"Doing right is never wrong."

"A chain is only as strong as its weakest link."

"If you don't watch out for yourself no one else will."

"If you get something for nothing that is usually what it's worth."

"Don't burn your bridges behind you."

"Failure is one thing you can achieve without much effort."

The philosophy of dealing with the situations life tosses at you flavored some of our grandparents' advice. Sometimes a touch of humor was used to drive the point home. They used to say:

"Fool me once, shame on you; fool me twice, shame on me."

"Time heals all wounds."

"The problems of this life are meant to make us better, not bitter."

"Speech is silver; silence is golden."

"Gems cannot be polished without friction."

Sometimes our grandparents recited sermons in miniature. They used to say:

"Honesty is the best policy."

"The hardest part of any job is getting started."

"A journey of a thousand miles begins with the first step."

"Beauty is only skin deep."

"Beauty is in the eye of the beholder."

Often small happenings were used to predict coming events. Those predictions were taken quite seriously and, believe it or not, often came true. They used to say:

"If your right hand itches you will get money. If your left hand itches, you will meet somebody new."

"If your nose itches, someone is coming to visit."

When the old dominecker rooster crowed right on your doorstep at the break of day, they used to say, "It is a true sign you will have unexpected company" that day.

When white puffs of clouds appeared in a clear blue summer sky, they used to say, "The shepherd is taking his flock in because within 24 hours it's going to rain."

If, when looking at the big dipper, it appears to be tilted, it's a sign there will be rain because,

they used to say, "A tilted dipper spills out water."

Our grandparents used things around them to express feelings, to give advice. They used to say:

"Too many cooks spoil the broth."

"A watched pot never boils."

"If you want to have bread, you can't loaf."

"Don't count your chickens before they're hatched."

"The worst wheel does the most squeaking."

"The squeakiest wheel gets the axle grease."

"A strong wind makes a strong tree."

Some of their quaint sayings reflected the speech patterns of that time. Some, while they made sense to folks back then, might cause us to scratch our heads nowadays. One such saying was: "A whistling girl and a crowing hen will come to no good end." *(Editor's Note: A girl who whistled was viewed as demonstrating masculine attributes, much as a crowing hen. The crowing hen usually ended up in a stew pot; most felt a whistling girl would never find a good husband.)*

"Many hands make light work."

"There's learning in doing."

"Busy people don't have time to be busybodies."

Another very old saying that my 87-year-old Aunt Lilly still uses is: "Promises and pie crusts were both made to be broken." She used that one on a U.S. senator to make him keep a political promise. And it worked!

Coming from the Appalachian Mountains are some unusual sayings with a rhythm all their own. A farmer who wanted to indicate that something was of little value might say, "It won't pull worth a team of mules." Some of their speech was poetry itself. Is there any lovelier way to say something lasts a long time than to say it is "forever and enduring"? And if it has been quite awhile since an event, it was described as having been "a time and a time."

The sayings of yesterday often carry with them a message not limited to the times in which they were spoken, but can enrich our lives in these modern times. That wisdom is not locked into a certain era. It is available to us now, but it is up to us to truly listen to the subtle meanings behind the short phrases and permit that wisdom to enhance our life today. We can learn so much by really listening to what they used to say. ❖

Grandma Said So

By June Marie Schasre

My Grandma Eichler possessed some of the most outrageous beliefs. However, when I was a little girl in upstate New York, I took her pronouncements seriously. So did a lot of other people. Whatever Grandma said must be so. After all, she was the one who nursed all her children through bouts of measles and whooping cough, and she was the sage who knew how to make dough plasters that would draw out an infection when placed on a wound.

I would have continued to believe her notions had it not been for my grandfather. He managed to dispute most of her beliefs—if not within her earshot, at least by muttering under his breath.

When, for example, Grandma came out with a remark like, "Fat men are always good-natured," Grandpa muttered, "They have to be, because if they get into an argument, they can't run as fast as the other guy."

One of my favorites was, "The best way to get rid of warts is to bury a dead cat by the light of the moon." To that, Grandpa secretly replied, "Certainly it will—provided the warts are on the cat!"

I recall more of Grandma's sayings than Grandpa's retorts. Perhaps you will think up some Grandpa-like responses of your own to challenge these sacred beliefs.

I recall more of Grandma's sayings than Grandpa's retorts. Most of them were based in her grassroots education on the family farm. Some reflected the wisdom of folks raised closer to nature. Some seemed a bit far-fetched to me. Perhaps you will think up some Grandpa-like responses of your own to challenge these sacred beliefs.

Grandma's Greatest Bits of Infinite Wisdom

- An apple a day keeps the doctor away.
- Thunder causes milk to turn sour.
- Your hair may turn white overnight from fright.
- Long slender hands indicate an artistic temperament.
- A dough plaster draws the poison out of wounds.
- You will experience growing pains as you grow.
- If a cinder blows in your eye, remove it by rubbing the other eye.
- Cats kill babies by sucking their breath out.
- A pearl necklace loses its shine if the wearer is ill.
- Aluminum cooking pans cause cancer.
- If a shingles rash encircles your body you will die.
- A high forehead indicates great intelligence.
- White eggs are better than brown.
- If you have cold hands, it means you have a warm heart.
- If you touch a toad you will get warts.

- A rag soaked in vinegar wrapped tightly around the forehead will relieve a sick headache.
- Feed a cold and starve a fever.
- If you place a newborn baby on its left side, he or she will be left-handed.
- An hour of sleep before midnight is worth two hours afterward.
- Fish is brain food.
- An expectant mother has to eat enough for two.
- Lines in the palms of your hands foretell the future.
- If a pregnant woman wears high heels she will have a cross-eyed baby.
- If you cut your hair often it will grow in thicker.
- A child who grinds his or her teeth while sleeping has worms.
- Red hair signifies a hot temper.
- Brains and beauty never go together.
- It is not good to eat fish and drink milk at the same meal.
- A square jaw indicates a stubborn person.
- Crazy people get worse during a full moon.
- You can become bald by wearing a hat indoors.
- To remove a cinder from your eye, blow your nose on the opposite side.
- A drowning person rises to the surface of the water three times before actually drowning.
- Grape seeds cause appendicitis.
- Birthmarks are caused by the expectant mother seeing something frightening.
- A mother loses a tooth for every child she bears.
- If you cut a baby's hair before taking him to the barbershop, he will die.
- A sty can be cured by rubbing the eye with a gold ring.
- Carrying a whole nutmeg in your pocket prevents seasickness.
- Bread is less fattening when toasted.
- A baby who walks before he is a year old will grow up bow-legged.
- Whiskey is the best antidote for snakebite.

Grandpa always contradicted this last belief. He invariably asked, "Do you pour the whiskey on the bite, or do you drink it?"

Looking back, I do believe Grandpa was a highly intelligent man to have questioned Grandma's beliefs. After all, he did have a high forehead! ❖

A Prayer for Our Times

By Orin L. Crain

Slow me down, Lord!

Ease the pounding of my heart by the quieting of my mind. Steady my hurried pace with a vision of the eternal reach of time.

Give me, amidst the confusion of my day, calmness of the everlasting hills. Break the tension of my nerves with the soothing music of the singing streams that live in my memory.

Help me to know the magical restoring power of sleep. Teach me the art of taking minute vacations … of slowing down to look at a flower, to chat with an old friend or make a new one, to pat a stray dog, to watch a spider build a web, to smile at a child, or to read a few lines from a good book.

Remind me each day that the race is not always to the swift; that there is more to life than increasing its speed. Let me look upward into the branches of the towering oak and know that it grew great and strong because it grew slowly and well.

Slow me down, Lord, and inspire me to send my roots deep into the soil of life's enduring values, that I may grow toward the stars of my greater destiny. ❖

Plant Happiness

Author Unknown

First, plant five rows of "peas":
Prayer,
Perseverance,
Politeness,
Promptness,
Purity.
Next, plant three rows of "squash":
Squash gossip,
Squash criticism,
Squash indifference.
Then, five rows of "lettuce":
Let us be faithful to duty,
Let us be unselfish,
Let us be truthful,
Let us follow Christ,
Let us love one another.
No garden is complete without "turnips":
Turn up for church,
Turn up with a smile,
Turn up with new ideas,
Turn up with determination to make everything count for something good and worthwhile.

Bobo Knew Best

By Anna-Margaret O'Sullivan

"People may be poor," declared my grandmother in a tone that brooked no contradiction, "but there is no excuse for not being scrupulously clean." This was one of her favorite pronouncements.

It was bath time back in the 1920s. My brother, sister and I had each been popped into a galvanized washtub holding a few inches of hot, soapy water. Wielding her washcloth like a Brillo pad, our grandmother (called Bobo by her grandchildren) moved from one tub to the next. Her washrag abraded knees and elbows so vigorously that I halfway expected a gleam of white bone to appear on our knobby joints.

"Please, Bobo," I begged. "Couldn't we just be clean without being scrupulously clean?" I figured the difference between the two lay between the epidermis, which had no feeling, and the dermis, which did. Her soapy cloth was already attacking the dermis. My piteous plea amused all my hearers but one. My grandmother's reply was a crisp, "Cleanliness is next to godliness."

Bobo had a proverb, a quotation or a statement of family policy for every imaginable occasion. Undoubtedly, the principles she helped my mother instill in her grandchildren became the foundation of our characters in adult life.

"Don't cheat. An honest D, or even an F, is better than a dishonest A."

"It's a disgrace to return a neighbor's dish empty."

"Always return more than you borrowed." Accordingly, when my grandmother returned Mrs. Banta's plate, she sent a piece of apple pie to replace the wedge of chocolate cake it had held the day before. Our family didn't hold with borrowing, and it was shameful to be known as a "borrower," but emergencies did come up. Mother sent a cup-and-a-half of sugar to replace the level cupful she had borrowed from Mrs. Carson, who meticulously sent back the extra half-cup.

When our upstairs bedrooms resembled an adjunct to the town dump, my grandmother's favorite motto was, "A place for everything and everything in its place." Such an ideal was, and to this day is, beyond me. Neatniks march to a different drummer.

One evening, we called on some acquaintances in the village. To my sister and me, their house was unbelievable. All the way home, my grandmother marveled aloud at such a phenomenon. "Everything in its place! Not a toy in sight! You'd never know a child lived there."

"Mama," exclaimed my mother with a burst of spirit, "you may admire that, but I don't. If a child lives there, I want to see toys in sight, books, crayons—something that says it's a child's home as well as his parents'."

My grandmother was astonished and more than a little miffed to have her values questioned. There was a lot to be said for perfect order, of course (and she said so), but for the rest of my life I remembered the distinction Mother made between a house and a home.

Most children who can print their names do so in all sorts of places. One day, our names appeared on the dusty pane of a window looking out onto the porch from the front room. The three of us were promptly informed that "fools' names, like their faces, are always seen in public places," and given the task of washing the window and our dusty fingertips.

I never quite figured out that saying, since the faces of the leading denizens of our village appeared regularly in the post office, the store, the garage, the confectionery and the two local churches. Surely, such respectable places weren't full of "fools' faces"!

Nor did I comprehend why my shrill attempts to whistle a tune at the age of eight led to an ominous prophecy: "A whistling girl and a crowing hen always come to some bad end." Why was whistling so reprehensible for me, but not for my brother or the man who brought the milk at 5:30 in the morning?

Occasionally, with astonishing results, repeated admonitions fell on fertile ground. "Vanity! All is vanity!" "Pride goeth before a fall." "Pretty is as pretty does." "As a man thinketh in his heart, so is he."

New clothes in the 1920s and 1930s were so hard to come by that any we were lucky enough to get were highly prized. During one particular Lenten season, I was eagerly saving a new dress to wear to church on Easter Sunday. Then, conscience gave me a vicious jab. Vanity! Pride! Could it be that flaunting my fine feathers was more important to me than celebrating a holy Easter?

At the last minute, when everybody else had gone without me, I made a decision. Regretfully leaving the new dress in my closet, I went to church in a dress Mother had starched 'til it rattled, but which was now a faded blue.

My grandmother hadn't bargained for so literal an interpretation of her principles. She was furious. With the means to do so, I had failed to "keep up appearances," and of all times, on Easter Sunday!

The heavens fell. In my naïveté, it had not occurred to me until this moment that anyone but God would notice or care. I was still sure that among all those Easter furbelows, nobody had wasted a second glance at the only shabby worshiper in the church. Common sense whispered that my "scrupulously clean" cotton frock, faded though it was, couldn't really have disgraced the family forever. Any minute now, I'd recall the proverb I needed. It was one of my grandmother's favorites, and I was pretty sure it would prove that at least my intention was linked with godliness. ❖

> *"Couldn't we just be clean without being scrupulously clean?"*

Grandpa's Sayings

By Robert E. Crawford

My grandpa, Tom Runyon, had a lot of sayings and remarks. When someone at the little country church remarked that his clothes didn't fit, he replied, "You can't tell how much hay a man can pitch by th' way his overalls hang."

Referring once to a young lady who lived up the road that "put on airs," Grandpa said, "Th' apple that's the hardest to reach ain't necessarily th' sweetest."

Of course, I've forgotten more of Grandpa's sayings than I remember, but over the years I've recalled quite a few.

We were climbing into the wagon after church one Sunday, and Mom said, "Pap, how'd you like th' preachin'?"

Grandpa's reply was a classic. "He could have plowed deeper if he didn't try to do th' whole farm."

One time when I nearly fell out of the wagon, Grandpa grabbed my "galluses," saying, "Son, don't unhitch th' saddle while you're still in it."

Grandpa's dry, humorous remarks were intended to teach lessons about life. "Principles," he called 'em. With him, the whole of mankind's behavior was a bunch of principles.

For instance, "You can't tell how a dog will hunt by the way he wags his tail." What Grandpa was really saying was, "Don't judge an individual by outward signs of enthusiasm." Or maybe he meant, "What appears to be, may be an illusion." Or was it, "It's the results that matter, not the promise"?

I guess I don't remember as many of Grandpa's sayings as I want to, but a lot of his principles have guided my life. He was not an educated man, but he was smart.

As Grandpa would say, "Sometimes a poorly cow gives th' sweetest milk." ❖

Letter to a Bride

By Betty Schumack

While sorting through some old letters and mementos, I came across this letter from a very close cousin, written in 1946, just a few weeks before my wedding. We were both under 21 years of age, and I was very touched and amused at some of the sage advice given by a bride of only one year herself. I believe most of these thoughts are very typical of the young, idealistic American bride at that time. In this day of prenuptial agreements, it's fun to look back to the time when young couples married for love and enjoyed even the hard times.

Dear Bubbins;

I just got your letter this morning and golly, I'm so excited about your wedding coming up! You'd think I was doing it all over again myself. I'm so happy for you. How I wish I could be there for the happy occasion. I bet your folks are really in a dither now … busy as bees. Is your dad nervous?

You'll be a pretty bride, and I'd love to be right there, but I can't, so if you'll write and tell me just what time you'll be married and all that, I'll subtract one hour from our time, and I'll walk right up as far as the altar with you … make-believe, anyway.

Just think! Three weeks from tomorrow and you'll be married! I hope you can have a honeymoon, even if it's just a day. Make it a honeymoon you'll never forget. We had only three days in the mountains, and we just climbed rocks, went swimming and drove around, but we'll never forget it. Just think, I've been a married woman for a little over a year now. I've got the swellest guy in the world. Boy! I couldn't have done better if I had built him myself! We really have a lot of fun. I like married life; there's nothing like it!

Say, that little house you rented sounds super. You will have such fun fixing it up the way you want it. And those little inconveniences you spoke of (the outdoor bathroom and water pump) won't be inconveniences at all. Ten years from now you'll have a picnic talking about your first house. Life, I guess, is just what you want to make it. If you have your mind made up to be happy, well, there isn't anything stronger than that. Just you and him … against the whole wide world.

They say, "The first year is the hardest." That's a lot of baloney! If it is true, I'm sure going to be a happy girl the rest of my life, and you'll say the same thing. Personally, we didn't see any great change. There's nothing to it. All anyone has to remember is, "I surrender, Dear," and, "Don't go to sleep on an argument." You do that, and you won't honestly be able to say you've ever

In other words, I guess I'm just saying I wouldn't be single again for all the tea in China, and you've got to be just as happy and thoroughly satisfied as I am.

had an argument—
just discussions.
We always talk over everything.
Don't ever bottle up, whether good or bad.
Say what you think, but be sure you mean it.

Oh, married life is super! You've got someone you can tell everything to, lean on and dream with. It's a big step, but it's certainly no funeral!

We spent a week in a hotel before we could get into our apartment, then we moved and had our first meal in our new home. We each washed a plate, cup and saucer, and had scrambled eggs and coffee with doughnuts for dessert, amid all of our boxes and dirty scrub rags, but oh, what fun!

Our first two nights, we didn't have any pillows or sheets, only a blanket, but it was summer. His mother was sending us four sheets and we didn't get them in time, but we still wanted to stay in our apartment, so we did without them. We'll never forget all of those little things. Some people would say, "Oh, how awful!" but it wasn't.

There was just he and I together, and what a good feeling. It's something no one can take away from you, no matter what happens or how tough things get sometimes (it's not all honey and cake). But no matter, you've still got him, and that's important because you've had your names together in heaven since the day you were born.

In other words, I guess I'm just saying I wouldn't be single again for all the tea in China, and you've got to be just as happy and thoroughly satisfied as I am.

You've probably heard this before, but I would highly suggest that you go to a good middle-aged country doctor and say, "I'm going to be married, and I want to know what you've got to tell me." Now, you'll say, "I've heard about the birds and the bees before." I had, too. Every married girl I knew told me everything she knew. The only thing is, I heard so many things, I didn't know who was right or what was what. I was about to agree that I would be transformed the minute I said, "I do." So I went to the doctor and he talked, and I listened and asked questions. If I were you, I would take $5 off your wedding dress and put it on a doctor bill. I think it is that important. All in all, it's highly educational!

Getting married is fun, isn't it? Being married is more fun, though. Afterwards, don't forget your budget. We found out that you can't get any place at all if you don't budget somewhat; this much for groceries, and so much for rent. It's even fun proving to yourself that you can make and stick to one of those awful things. Even 25 cents leftover makes you so tickled, you'll probably think it is $25 instead.

Oh, I know you'll be happy and get along fine, and soon you can wait for a baby, like we are now. What a glorious feeling! My doctor tells me I'm not doing anything spectacular, but I think he's wrong.

Enough said from an ol' married lady. I'm sure you'll have a nice honeymoon, and it doesn't matter where you are … you won't care anyway. Just enjoy yourselves … that's a honeymoon!

Have a nice wedding, and a wonderful, wonderful married life. Write to us when you come back down to earth and good luck! We're betting on you!

Bye and Love, Cousin Norma

A Short Course in Human Relations

Submitted by Mrs. Victor J. Henderson

The most important six words:
"I admit I made a mistake."

The most important five words:
"I am proud of you."

The most important four words:
"What is your opinion?"

The most important three words:
"Would you mind?"

The most important two words:
"Thank you."

The most important word: "Please"
Another most important word: "We"
The least important word: "I"

Jim Daly
©
1988

Mama's Credo for Living

By Esther Orenstein

Mama's lovely hazel eyes held mine fast as she spoke; they were bright with unshed tears and my guilt lay mirrored in their reflection. I thought for the zillionth time, *What makes me do these awful things? Why do I always hurt Mama, when I love her so?*

Mama's words came more in sorrow than in anger. "Lying is a sin, Esther, a sin against God. You sinned and you were punished."

There were no shadings in Mama's rainbow. Her philosophy and faith in God were absolute. Things were good or bad, black or white. There were no grays at all. But Mama never figured on her youngest child—me. Lonely and rebellious at being left on my own while Mama worked at the local factory, I looked for attention wherever and whenever I could find it.

My sister was 12, a world away from 8, and she wanted no part of taking care of me. Occasionally she bribed me with her daily penny for spending so that I would keep out of her way while she played with her friends.

I can still hear the reverberating echoes of constant scoldings with amazing clarity, but at the time, they fell on deaf ears. My adult mind flinches at the memory of how many meetings there were between my sore and tender backside with the flat of Mama's hand. But I never seemed to learn. The next day, there I was, looking for mischief.

Mama kissed me goodbye as I left for school. "Put on your stocking cap, Esther. It's bitter cold outside and I want your ears covered."

"Yes, Mama. See, I've got it on." I flew out of the house, with the devil close behind, whispering in my ear. Off came the varicolored cap that Mama had knitted for me while she rocked by the warmth of the kitchen stove in the evening, after a hard day's work in the factory. I was ashamed of it because it wasn't store-bought, like the other kids'. What did I know of Mama's anguish later that week, when I lay sick and feverish with abscessed ears, the direct result of my false and prickly pride? How little I realized how badly we needed the money lost at work while she stayed home to take care of me!

And what did I know of the sacrifice Mama made as she clunked pennies and nickels into an empty tin can, change saved to become a doll carriage for my birthday? I was a tomboy and carriages were for sissy girls. Unfeelingly, I stripped it, leaving only the base and the wheels and the handle. It made a fantastic scooter—much more sensible to me than a carriage—but Mama couldn't see it that way. She was very angry.

"If I wanted you to have a scooter (swat), I'd have bought you a scooter (swat), and not a doll carriage (swat)."

Or the time I sold the sour pickles right out from under Mama's nose. They stood in our back hall in a big, wooden barrel—a goodly winter's supply gleaned from last summer's garden. Day after day, I lined up my friends in the back hall and wheedled their pennies out of them in return for a sour pickle. At night, shivering with cold and anticipation, I huddled under the feather quilt and counted my ill-gotten gains.

Of course, Mama was quick to notice the dwindling supply of pickles and, knowing who the culprit was, she lost no time in applying punishment to fit the crime. For days, chairs were not for sitting. Punished, and my wealth confiscated, I somehow lost my taste for business ventures and pickles. Pickles and I still aren't on eating terms.

With Papa in a tuberculosis sanatorium and the death of a lovely teenage daughter fresh in Mama's grieving heart, I used to wonder from where she drew her strength and fortitude. When I grew older, it was plain to see.

Mama was a tiny woman, but only in physical

As I listened to Mama's words, spoken softly and in complete faith. They struck at my childish heart like nothing ever before.

stature. In heart and in mind, and in her faith in God, Mama stood tall. She met each day with calm and hope and grace.

Long before daybreak, Mama was tiptoeing in the darkness of the kitchen, poking the dying coals in the ageless black stove, cajoling a little warmth into the house before it was time for me to get up for school. When winter ran to meet the gentle springtime, Mama still rose before dawn and took care of the house and worked in the garden until it was time for her to leave for work.

I remember those days now, and wonder at the innocent cruelty of children. I'm sure I didn't mean to be bad and always get into trouble. Grown, I agonized over the things I had done and the heartaches I had caused Mama, and I wished over and over again that I could tell her how sorry I was. But when I was grown, it was too late. Mama was gone.

That fateful day of my great sin was warm and sweet, and the promise of golden, sun-drenched summertime wafted in the air like a rare and heady wine. Rows of maple trees outside my school window wore their almost-green leaves like a crown. My nostrils filled with the smell of the hearth and it was good. Maybe God looked down upon his world and was pleased, and so rewarded us with that perfect day, a day of haunting beauty that stays imprinted on the memory forever.

My mind hopscotched as I wiggled in my seat and watched white puffs skim across the azure sky. I dreamed of the free and unfettered world outside the school. Dimly, I heard Miss Johnson talking about long division.

"Miss Siegel, M-i-s-s S-i-e-g-e-l! Do you think you could rejoin the class? I'm waiting for your answer."

I mumbled an excuse for not knowing and sat back to dream again, while my classmate answered correctly. *Ah,* I thought impatiently, *when will that 3 o'clock bell ring? There's little enough time for me to play, and today is a perfect day for aggies, or ollie-ollie-in-come-frees or new cucumbers—not for long division. Maybe I'll have time to go to my tree house and play the game of make-believe.*

Eight was an age of innocence for me; an age

when childish dreams were still hugged close. They made life beautiful. Tall for my age, and lanky, with legs that stumbled in their haste and arms always looking for a place to set, gangling and awkward in body, I dreamt of beauty. One magical day, I'd have lovely clothes to wear—and they wouldn't be hand-me-downs—and my black, Dutch-clipped hair that I hated so would become blond and curly, and I'd be pretty and no more a tomboy, and never cause trouble for Mama. Ah, how I dreamed in that tree house!

The next day, hopscotching on, my mind went on to school. This beautiful day, the thought of school was unbearable. *What, I thought, what if just this once I played hooky? Mama would never know, because I'll write a note and sign her name, and tomorrow I'll give it to the teacher. Nobody will know but me.* I scribbled the note while courage was still fresh, and signed Mama's name, and stuffed it in my dress pocket, ready for tomorrow's lie.

The dark deed done, I danced home helter-skelter, dreaming of a whole day with nothing to do but play. Dropping my books on the nearest chair, I grabbed my bag of aggies and dashed out to do business. I found myself alone. My frenzied mind, tangled in its web of lies, forgot that the other kids on the block went to school, too.

I sat on the stoop and sulked, and agonized over my folly. And then I remembered the square of the nearby town. Of course! That would be the most wonderful thing to do, better than aggies or anything!

With my decision made, my heart and feet leap-frogged all the way, racing to that magical place. It was only a mile from home, but the streets were enormously wide and teeming with traffic, even in those long-ago days, and I wasn't allowed to go there alone.

The public library was there, with its ancient ivy swarming over the warm red bricks on the outside and its wonderful books on the inside. The local museum was there, very small, but to a child, tremendous; and the duck pond was there, right in the middle of the square, with ducklings swimming without concern, while horses went by them. The pond was manmade, but did I care? It was perfect.

All the trappings for a child's delight were there, the best one being that it was forbidden fruit. It challenged me and I picked up the challenge.

I was almost there, and in an agony of impatience I started across the street without looking. I heard the ugly screech of snarling brakes and, in the split second before the car slammed into me, my childish mind cried, *What will I tell Mama? Oh God, what can I tell Mama? I'm supposed to be in school!*

The car tossed me like a leaf before a fierce autumn wind and I rolled over and over on the unrelenting cement. A policeman came and hovered over me and spoke kind words. The ambulance clanged its way to the accident while people gathered around and murmured, "Poor kid, poor little kid." The voices made their way to me through a smothering blanket of pain, but above them I imagined Mama's voice. I had done bad things, but I had never been in trouble like this.

Why were you bad again, Esther? Why did you lie? What's to become of you, Esther? Each thought pricked my conscience and I prayed for oblivion.

Harried, overworked, wonderful Mama was notified at work and she came running. After all the years, it still hurts to remember the look of fear for her child on her face.

My clothes, torn and bloodied from the accident, were given to Mama, and crumpled in my dress pocket she discovered my lie.

She didn't say a word. Night after night, Mama came to visit me after work. She sat by my side and coaxed me to eat and talked to me about my friends and how much they missed me. Her ebony hair, winged with gray, fell in wisps about her strained and tired face. That gentle, gentle face! But she talked and smiled and encouraged me with loving words.

"You'll see, Honey, soon the whole thing will be a bad dream. You'll be home and everything will be the way it always was."

Each night Mama brought me something special—a big, round navel orange, or my favorite kind of doughnut, or a little celluloid doll from the five-and-dime that she had dressed in clothes made with her care-worn hands.

I was young and my broken bones healed quickly. Every day Mama saw progress and was buoyed by it, and each day my guilt grew. It stifled me. I began to understand the grief I had caused Mama. I ached to pour out my confession; I was suddenly afraid Mama would never believe anything I ever said again, and I wanted another chance.

It came on my first day home from the hospital. That evening, in my own bed at last, surrounded by all the dear familiar sights I had always taken for granted, Mama spoke.

"When will you learn, Esther, that it's wrong to lie? I've told you over and over again, lying is a sin—a sin against God. You sinned and you were punished."

I cried bitter tears of remorse as I listened to Mama's words, spoken softly and in complete faith. They struck at my childish heart like nothing ever before. Like lightning racing across a summer sky, they made me see. And seeing, I was never quite the same again.

The intervening years have softened the hurt, but Mama's credo for living has given great meaning to my adult life. The memory of her gentle ways and her faith in God are what Mama left me as a legacy, and I pray that legacy will always be my guide. ❖

Basic Training of the Golden Rule

Field Newspaper Syndicate

If you open it—close it.
If you turn it on—turn it off.
If you unlock it—lock it.
If you break it—repair it.
If you can't fix it—call in
someone who can.
If you borrow it—return it.
If you use it—take good care of it.
If you make a mess—clean it up.
If you move it—put it back.
If it belongs to someone else and
you want to use it—get permission.
If you don't know how
to operate it—leave it alone.
If it doesn't concern you—
don't mess with it.
If you're ever in doubt—ask.

If I Had My Life to Live Over

If I had my life to live over, I would go to school a bit longer. (I went three days in my brother's place once when he was sick. We looked so much alike that the teacher didn't know the difference!)

If I had my life to live over, I would buy for my wonderful son a baseball and bat, and a football, and I'd take him fishing now and then instead of working 16 hours a day, year after year. And maybe I'd buy him a Shetland pony.

If I had my life to live over, maybe I'd buy my lovely daughter a big doll buggy while she was little instead of buying her a little one after she got big. (I didn't know then that daughters noticed such things.) And I just might buy her a silk graduation dress!

If I had my life to live over, I would try to find a way to finance a week's vacation together for my family once each year.

If I had my life to live over, I would find enough time and money—somehow—to take my family out to dinner at least once a month, even if it did cost $5 for the four of us. (My children never knew restaurants served anything but hamburgers until they were in their late teens!)

If I could turn back the pages of time, I would lose less sleep worrying over things that never happened.

I would read more fine print and sign fewer dotted lines.

I would live, laugh and love more—and gripe less.

I would listen more and talk less.

I would tell my wife "I love you" at the end of each day. And I'd gather more daisies!

—Bert Crampton

Good Manners

By Audrey Corn

When it came to her children's manners, Mama demanded the best. She didn't much care whether I knew the proper way to eat an artichoke. Truth to tell, when I was growing up back in the 1940s, none of us had ever seen an artichoke.

Mama's concerns were more practical. She taught my sister and me about courtesy, respect and kindness. Jennie and I learned to say "Please" and "Thank you."

Our conversations were punctuated with "sirs" and "madams." We knocked before we entered a room, and we held the door for the person behind us.

As for table manners, forget the artichokes. Mama was happy if we chewed with our mouths shut.

Mama tried to explain the difference between lies and tact. When I was a child, I couldn't always make the distinction. Some days, I still can't.

Our good manners may have looked charming and unrehearsed to outsiders, but believe me, they did not come naturally. Every "please" and every "thank you" was a tribute to Mama's determination and patience.

I remember the heated arguments we had over kissing. Some grown-ups wanted us to kiss them hello and goodbye. Mama explained that it was rude to refuse.

Aunt Ella was the hardest to kiss. She was really Papa's aunt and, looking back, I'm sure she was a kind, well-meaning lady. Unfortunately, Aunt Ella reeked of garlic. She wore a little pouch of the stinky stuff underneath her blouse to ward off every imaginable illness.

The minute Aunt Ella spotted us at a family gathering, she would ask for her kiss. Mama, who was born with good manners, stepped right up, but Jennie and I hung back as long as we dared.

Early on, Papa devised his own strategy for keeping his aunt at bay. Whenever we visited with Aunt Ella, Papa had a cold. Or he was coming down with a cold. Or he was just getting over a cold. Papa would blow his nose a couple of times and fake a dry cough, and Auntie seemed just as happy to skip his kiss.

One day I lied and told Aunt Ella that I had a cold. Mama bit her lip and didn't say a word. However, after Auntie left, Mama delivered a long lecture about honesty and respect, and she took away my movie privileges for the following Saturday.

I pleaded and I wept. I vowed eternal honesty. I promised that from that day forward I would rush up to Auntie and kiss her the minute she walked through our front door.

But Mama held firm. I spent Saturday afternoon at home while all my friends, including Jennie, saw *Meet Me in St. Louis*. To compound my misery, the film starred Margaret O'Brien.

Not long after that, one of our neighbor ladies dropped by with a plate of home-baked brownies. Mama poured me a glass of milk and let me sample one. "Do you like it?" the neighbor lady asked.

I remembered the lie told to Aunt Ella and the punishment it brought. "Mama's brownies taste better," I said. From the look on my mother's face, I knew I was in hot water—again.

"But you said to be honest!" I protested after the neighbor lady went home.

Mama tried to explain the difference between lies and tact. When I was a child, I couldn't always make the distinction. Some days, I still can't.

As I grew older, Mama addressed her lessons to more controversial issues. Her notions of appropriate clothing for young ladies did not always coincide with my own. Little girls (13 was still little) did not wear black. Little girls did not wear lipstick. They did not rouge their cheeks, nor did they paint their fingernails.

Ladies put on hats and gloves for formal outings. Ladies did not appear in public with— shudder!—curlers in their hair or bedroom slippers on their feet.

Above all, ladies did not use cuss words. Their language was clean, their thoughts were pure and when their undergarments tore, they never resorted to safety pins. A lady was handy with a needle and thread.

Of course, I argued with Mama, but she made it clear that in our family, she was the final arbiter of good manners. When I was old enough, she assured me, I could set my own standards.

Eventually, I did grow older, but by then I had internalized Mama's values. I chew with my mouth closed. I try to be tactful. I dutifully kiss my relatives and I'm proud to say that I don't even own a safety pin.

There's just one rule that I break with depressing regularity. Unbelievable as it would seem to Mama, there is not a single millinery shop within shopping distance. Even the most fashionable ladies from the finest families go about their formal duties without hats.

This strikes me as sad because, as Mama often said, folks who look like ladies and gentlemen usually act like them. Just one more reason why I miss the Good Old Days. ❖

Sensible Speech

By Madeliene Daniels

When I was growing up, the older folks in my life had a very expressive, terse, to-the-point way of speaking. There was never any doubt as to what they meant. They were not averse to comparing people, young and old, to whatever came to mind. I don't believe they could have talked without using the names of animals, birds, flowers, insects and food. It came as naturally to them as breathing.

Grandma was always able to explain every mood of Grandpa's. Sometimes he was "as mad as a hornet," "as cross as a bear" or "more bark than bite." Other times, he was "as frisky as a colt," "full of ginger" or "proud as a peacock." He could never get out of hand; she would never let him.

Someone who provoked Grandma could be "sour as a pickle," "an old windbag," "silly as a goose" or "ugly as an old mud fence." Such things were never said in their hearing, of course. Her feelings assuaged, she usually reversed it all by saying the person in question was really just "as harmless as a dove."

As far as little children were concerned, they could be "as cute as a button," "knee-high to a grasshopper" or "growing like a weed."

She had a tender spot for young girls. They invariably were as "pretty as a picture," "fresh as a daisy," "shy as a violet" or "sweet as honey." The girls in the neighborhood enjoyed being around her; she made them feel special and pretty, even if they were not.

Sometimes Grandma took her turn. If the washing was not as white as she expected, she could be "as mad as an old wet hen." She said so herself! We liked her best the days she said she was as "happy as a lark" and proved it by baking an extra batch of cookies.

When it rained, older folks generally said it was "raining cats and dogs." For awhile, I took that literally and watched for them, but I soon learned better. Other times, they said it was "raining pitchforks," or "coming down in buckets." Anyway, no matter what they said, we children came to understand that it was raining extra hard and we always scurried for cover.

Other common expressions were: "the crack of dawn" (anyone worth his salt climbed out of bed at that time), "high noon," "the black of night" and "the dead of winter." I always shivered a little when I heard Grandma say "the dead of winter." She usually said it in January when it was cold and still, and everything was covered with snow.

One of my aunts was fond of saying, "A stitch in time saves nine," as she prodded us to learn the art of mending. And when I was lackadaisical about getting something done, I was usually told, "Don't put off until tomorrow what you can do today."

Grandpa said some men were "as strong as an ox" and could lift anything; others were "as weak as a kitten" and useless. He referred to little boys as "tadpoles." Grandma said some boys were "as awkward as cows" and others "as slow as turtles," especially when they knocked things over or the wood box wasn't filled on time.

Some people were "as poor as Job's turkey," but were high in Grandma's estimation because they were honest and did keep trying. "As honest as the day is long," she liked to say.

Other people had "the gift of gab" and "chattered like magpies" or "monkeys." All of us were

> *The old oddities that sprinkled the conversation of our elders are not much in use today. But they helped to teach solid values in life, and who is to say the method was wrong?*

John Slobodnik

warned about talking too much.

Other folks were "as busy as bees" and worked all the time. Undoubtedly, that applied to Grandma also because she never seemed to have an idle moment. She considered idleness "the devil's workshop."

The old oddities that sprinkled the conversation of our elders are not much in use today. But they helped to teach solid values in life, and who is to say the method was wrong? When Grandpa said, "Don't be so bullheaded," Johnny knew exactly what he meant. When Grandma said, "Pretty is as pretty does," a granddaughter knew at once that a grave error had been made and a change was in order. When Grandma said, "Fools step in where angels fear to tread," we knew we were really off the beam.

Habits of speech change with the times. Old forms are looked down upon as hackneyed, trite, crude and never used by "educated" people. But simple, plain, blunt, sensible speech had its use and certainly had merit for us farm kids. ❖

If You Say So, Mama

By Amelia E. Hitchings

My mama was a lady of picturesque speech. She was born over 100 years ago in the southeastern corner of Virginia, and even if your mother was born somewhere else, she might have used the same expressions. I use many of them today.

When she said a person had "gumption," she meant he had common sense and determination, or get-up-and-go. A lady dressed up fine and sashaying down the street was "Miss Priss," a "flibbertigibbet" who "wore her husband's salary on her back" and was "keeping his nose to the grindstone."

No one was ever merely poor, but "dead poor"; nor just dead, but "dead as a doornail"; nor neat, but "neat as a pin." And no person ever died, but he "keeled over and was dead and gone."

Anything broken was "in smithereens," "out of whack" and "kaflooey." A prominent person who didn't deserve the position was a "big dog" or a "high muckety-muck," or a "high-falutin' big shot."

Her remedy for a stubborn individual heading down the wrong path was to "let the cow kick him." Eventually he would "stew in his own juice" and that would be "a fine kettle of fish."

"Lickety-split" and "rip-roaring" meant too fast, while "rambunctious" and "frisky" meant exuberant. "Hobnobbing" indicated being seen with, and it had better not be with a "scalawag" or a "low-down hyena" or "skunk."

On a personal level, one's backside was a "bohunkas," and a girl too scantily clad was "showing everything she's got." A public toilet was a "comfort station." A person whose fat rippled when he walked was a "fatty-pipples," and

that was no put-down because Mama was fat herself. I guess she thought her corsets, which she wore daily, took care of the situation.

"Lay low" was her way of saying "Keep quiet about what you know," and when she said, "Make yourself scarce," I knew my absence was desired for a short while.

An old man's darling was his "sweet patootie" or his "tootsie-wootsie."

"Lollygagging" and "hemming and hawing" referred to standing around talking when one should be "getting down to brass tacks" and "striking while the iron's hot" to "take the bull by the horns."

A beauty shop term in the 1920s was "shampoo and finger-wave," which, in current usage, is rendered "wash and set." If Mama had no time to do a thorough job, she gave it "a lick and a promise."

An honest person was "true blue" and "on the up-and-up," whereas someone she suspected had "something up his sleeve" was "up to high jinks."

"Lambaste" threatened corporal punishment, as well as "what Paddy did to the drum," and "I'll bless you out."

"Lie down and lose yourself" was her way of saying, "Take a short nap," but someone in a deep sleep was "dead to the world."

"Full as a tick" described one who had eaten too much. "Back, back," was Mama's way of saying, "Put it in reverse." "All-fired" meant "totally," and when in trouble, one was "in the soup" or "floored."

When she made plans, it was always "if I live," or, "God being my helper." To encourage a person, she would say, "Buck up; don't be in the dumps."

A nicely dressed lady wore finery and was "fixy," but one overdressed was "all dolled up" and "flossy."

She would "put a bee in my bonnet" to "get down off my high horse" or "pay the piper" if I "didn't have a leg to stand on." Mama would "get her ducks in a row" and "rob Peter to pay Paul."

A high price was called "highway robbery" and she would say a salesman "held her up for a pretty penny" (but not often, I might add).

She would find "the lay of the land" before making a move. Being overworked meant being "run ragged," but "hunky-dory" indicated well-being, and when folks were sick, they were "flat-o'-the-back."

While proclaiming "there's many a slip 'twixt the cup and the lip," she advised me to "set my cap" for a certain boy, because she didn't want me to marry "any old Tom, Dick or Harry." She wanted a "humdinger" for a son-in-law. (She got one.)

A "whippersnapper" was a young person who behaved presumptuously. A "hullabaloo" was a big uproar, while "folderol" was a trifle or nonsense. "Rigamarole," was some complicated procedure. A " pig in a poke" was something you didn't want to buy without seeing.

I won't even try to define "fly-by-night," "will-o'-the-wisp," "get up off your haunches" or "the whole shebang."

Most of all, I loved Mama's comforting expressions: "You will come into your own, some sweet day"; "Stick to your guns"; "Your ship will come in by and by"; "Don't give up the ship"; "It will all blow over"; and "Sleep on it." These were soothing assurances.

I know a mother must correct her young in the early years, but she must comfort them in later years. And my mother's calming words still resound in my mind and heart to console and sustain me. ❖

Mama Would Have Said

By Hope LaShier

I can still remember Mama's humorous responses to life's problems. When our neighbor's pretty, intelligent daughter married the town drunk, Mama said, "She drove her geese to a poor market." When our hired hand married the rich Widow Brown, Mama said, "He found himself a bird nest on the ground." And the old man who married the young girl was described as either "looking for a purse or a nurse." In the old days, when a couple made a poor choice in marriage, their parents were apt to say, "You made your bed, now lie in it." The popular word today is "divorce."

When someone made a derogatory remark about someone, Mama would say, "That was the pot calling the kettle black." A sad person was described as, "Her face was as long as a clothesline," or, "She came dragging her tail feathers behind her."

In my 58 years of marriage, I have often said in a moment of crisis, "I only have two hands, and I'm wringing them both!" My dear mother-in-law would then calm me with her favorite adage, "Of all your troubles, great and small, the greatest of them don't happen at all."

Mama's sayings influenced Daddy, as well. He once spoke of a farmer who dressed in Western clothes and bragged about his ranch as being "all boots and no cattle."

With seven children in the family, Mama had a unique way of consoling our jealousy of the current "birthday child." She erased our sulking with, "Every dog has his day, and your day is coming." This taught me patience that has served me through the years.

When I was young, money was "as scarce as hen's teeth" (or so Mama said). When I signed up to sell 24 cans of Cloverine salve, I had the money spent before the order arrived through the mail. Mama told me, "Don't count your chickens before they hatch."

When Mama referred to politicians stumping, she said, "He did a fine job of fence sittin'." And when Mama served a light meal and the family finished eating quickly, she would say, "Short horse, easily curried."

I remember many more of Mama's humorous sayings. As for an adage of my own, I like, "When Mama died, she left the woodpile of humor a little higher." ❖

Weather Wisdom

It seems that all my life I have been defending the "old ways," particularly when it comes to use of signs from the natural world. Oh, it seems some folks don't mind if you're just interested in it, but if you're serious about it, you are hit from two fronts at once.

The first front are those who are a bit more scientifically minded. They might have a passing interest in these old customs, but let them think you're serious about it and they'll almost laugh you out of the room.

I remember one time discussing with one such scoffer the use of signs in the moon for determining the chance for precipitation. It had been pretty dry for quite a while, but I assured him that we would get a pretty good rain within the next couple of days.

"Why?" he asked.

"Can't you see the tilt of the crescent moon?" I responded. "It's ready to pour the water right out on this thirsty old earth!"

"Oh, c'mon!" he retorted. "You can't tell anything from looking at the moon. Anyway, it's like that every month."

"No, sometimes it lays on its back, holding the water in the crescent just like a dipper. At least that's the way my daddy taught me. Also, just look at that faint circle around the moon. That just confirms it. It'll rain—sure enough. Maybe tomorrow, but no doubt in the next couple of days."

He didn't believe my prognostication—or the moon's—not even when it came a toad strangler the next evening.

Now I have had some folks explain to me that there is a scientific explanation to why some of those signs work. I even had a discussion with a noted meteorologist one time who told me that the rain cycles definitely follow the moon cycles. That's all very interesting, but to this country boy the discussion about relative humidity, barometric pressures and jet streams is beyond me.

I just know how many times back on the farm that we used this weather wisdom to foretell bad storms, deep snows and the like. That was really important to us in the days when there was no local radio station for a quick severe weather alert, and when television was just a dream in somebody's mind.

The second front I have had to face is on the other end of the spectrum. These folks think that the use of such natural signs is some form of astrology or divination.

Now I'm a lay minister myself, and I have many times preached a sermon from Genesis 1 about the creation of the world. I have quoted verse 14 how on the fourth day He set the sun, moon and stars and said, "let them be for signs, and for seasons, and for days, and years…" I always figured that, if they were good enough for signs for Him, they ought to be good enough for me.

When Janice and I first envisioned this book, I immediately began to look forward to this chapter. I wanted to share with you stories of how old-timers in the Good Old Days were able to survive without benefit of modern forecasting. These stories include the nitty-gritty of what signs they looked for. They also include stories of heroism and courage in the face of natural catastrophes. Their stories of survival and coping are the greatest testimonials to their immense weather wisdom.

Janice and I still look for "sun dogs" and red skies and wooly worms and rain while the sun is shining today. We still plant our taters, onions, carrots and radishes by the dark of the moon, and our beans, peas, tomatoes and corn by the light of the moon.

We don't mind the scoffers or the doubters. We just keep applying those principles of weather wisdom we learned from our folks back in the Good Old Days.

—*Ken Tate*

Granddaddy's Weather Signs

By Lynne Stewart

*It ain't gonna rain no more,
no more.
It ain't gonna rain no more.
How in the heck will I wash my neck
If it ain't gonna rain no more?*

Granddaddy strummed his guitar and sang that ditty when he couldn't hear frogs croaking in the evening. He believed that frogs were quiet because it was going to be a dry summer. He also sang his bullfrog song:

*Bullfrog, bullfrog, won't croak tonight
Because there ain't no rain in sight.
Can't go fishin', the creek's gone dry.
And there's nary a cloud in the sky.
Bullfrog, sittin' on a lily pad,
Big rain's comin', then you'll be glad.*

Granddaddy saw weather signs in everything from carrots to smoke. A big catalpa tree in the yard was one of his weather indicators. Long, thick catalpa beans hanging on the tree meant a wet summer.

All through summer, he kept checking the bark on the trees in the yard. Heavier bark on the north side of a trunk meant there would be a lot of drifting snow that winter, especially if there was a thick growth of moss under the tree.

He looked for a cold winter if trees began shedding their leaves while still green, if the autumn sumac leaves were redder than usual, and if the summer grass was deep green. The greener the grass, the colder the winter.

He also predicted the weather by the moon. A ring around the moon meant a storm was brewing. When the horns of a crescent moon pointed down, it would rain within three days. If the horns pointed up, the next three days would be dry. In the evening we often sat on the porch and sang this song while Granddaddy played the guitar.

*Stand up, moon, point to the sky.
Pond's full up, creek's runnin' high.
Don't turn yourself upside down
And spill some water on the ground.
Moon, keep standin' right side up
And hold that water like a cup.
Stand up, moon, point to the sky.
Pond's full up, creek's runnin' high.*

Granddaddy predicted rain when smoke settled on the ground, but if smoke from the chimney rose straight up, the weather would be dry. He expected rain when leaves on trees and bushes turned over and showed their backs, when the bugs were thicker on the underside of hollyhock leaves, when cows were lying down in the pasture, when earthworms came up out of the ground, when dandelions grew thick in the yard, when he heard doves cooing or when he saw several ladybugs before noon.

When he heard a cricket somewhere in the house, he would say, "Cricket in the hall, heavy

Granddaddy's predictions were wrong more often than they were right, but he never stopped predicting the weather.

rainfall." If all these signs appeared on the same day, he began to worry about a cyclone.

The color of the evening sky was also a sign of the following day's weather. He said, "Evening sky gold, sunshine will hold. Evening sky gray, rain on the way."

Even the sleeping habits of our dogs and cats told him what to expect in the way of weather. He believed that when a dog slept on its stomach with its legs stretched out flat on the ground, a storm would blow in within 24 hours. But if the dog rolled over on its back with its legs in the air, there would be no rain the following day. This is the weather dog rhyme he recited:

Dog sticks
his legs up
toward the sky,
* You can*
bank on
tomorrow bein'
fair and dry.
* Dog's sleepin' on his belly.*
* Ma, get your umbrelly.*

If he found the cat asleep on something high off the ground, it was a sign of stormy weather ahead. When it rained on Easter Sunday, he expected rain to fall on the next seven Sundays.

Granddaddy believed we would have a bad winter if squirrels began gathering nuts in the middle of September, if they built their nests low in the trees and if their tails were unusually bushy.

Other signs of a long, hard winter were hornets building their nests close to the ground, spiders spinning webs on the south wall of the barn, a wide black band on a wooly worm's back, and tall ant hills: "When ants build high, snow's gonna fly."

If he heard owls hooting in October, he said,

"At Halloween time if the hoot owl hoots, you'll soon put on mittens and boots." Crows in a field could also indicate a bad winter: "Seven crows together bring in cold weather."

If we got more white eggs than brown ones for a week running, it meant a hail storm was coming. He also predicted hail when the cows spent a lot of time under the trees, when sparrows flew into the barn, or if he heard a screech owl: "Three days before it's hailing, owls screech like women wailing."

Fruit and vegetables also warned Granddaddy of a hard winter. Some of the signs he watched for were grapes maturing early, heavy blackberry blooms, tough sweet potato skins, thick corn silks, root vegetables such as parsnips and carrots growing deeper than usual, and too many seeds in watermelons. During the long, hot days of August, he would say, "For every day that's extra warm, there'll be a real bad winter storm."

He believed that the first 12 days after Christmas indicated what each month in the coming year would be like.

Granddaddy's predictions were wrong more often than they were right, but he never stopped predicting the weather. He was pleased when one of his weather forecasts proved to be correct and he always called it to our attention. When he was wrong he said nothing about it—and neither did anyone else in the family. We didn't want him to stop predicting the weather. We enjoyed all his weather rhymes and his songs, and he enjoyed being our weatherman. ❖

Granddaddy believed that frogs were quiet because it was going to be a dry summer.

When the Green Gits Back in the Trees

By James Whitcomb Riley

In spring, when the green gits back in the trees,
And the sun comes out and stays,
And yer boots pull on with a good tight squeeze
And you think of yer barefoot days;
When you ort to work and you want to not,
And you and yer wife agrees
It's time to spade up the garden lot—
When the green gits back in the trees—
Well, work is the least o' my ideas
When the green, you know, gits back in the trees!

When the green gits back in the trees, and bees
Is a buzzin' aroun' again,
In that kind of a lazy "go as you please"
Old gait they bum aroun' in'
When the groun's all bald where the hayrick stood,
And the crick's riz, and the breeze
Coaxes the bloom in the old dogwood,
And the green gits back in the trees,
I like, as I say, in sich scenes as these,
The time when the green gits back in the trees!

When the whole tail-feathers o' winter-time
Is all pulled out and gone.
And the sap it thaws and begins to climb,
And the sweat it starts out on
A feller's ferrerd, a-gittin down
As the old spring on his knees—
I kind o' like jes loafin' roun',
When the green gits back in the trees—
Jes' a-potterin roun' as I—durn—please—
When the green, you know, gits back in the trees. ❖

A Sign of Spring

By V.H. Sheppard

During the 1920s, when my sisters and I were growing up, we began looking for signs of spring soon after the Christmas holidays. While we impatiently awaited the first manifestation of spring, the groundhog always seemed to be working against us. He'd pop out every year if only for a moment and condemn us to six more weeks of winter confinement. Grandpa knew how anxious we were for spring to arrive and kept telling us, "Spring is just over the hill," but he never said what hill he had in mind.

Neither the red Jell-O and heart-shaped cakes on Valentine's Day nor the prospect of celebrating George Washington's birthday with cherry pie did much to quiet the restlessness we had begun to feel.

Before the first crocus pushed through the late snows to brighten our drab world or an early robin had hopped gingerly about over the still-frozen ground in search of food, we had used up just about all of our goodwill toward one another. Our discontentment lead to frequent squabbles and often to hair pulling and scratching.

Our fondest hope was to see our kite fly better than any other on the hill—to fly high and take our spirits soaring ...

It was a bad time for Mama, too. Her nerves were worn to a frazzle and she wished for spring even more than we did. Mama restored order by threatening to leave home. She would say, "I'm just going to walk off and let you kill each other."

That threat never failed to shame us. We needed Mama and didn't want her to go away and leave us, so we treaded lightly on the other's feelings and busied ourselves with some project. Among the things we turned our attention to was kite making.

In the little Michigan town where we spent our childhood, kites overhead marked the end of winter and the arrival of spring. In the spring, whenever I see a kite whipped into a frenzied gyration by gusts of wind, I remember the hill just outside of town dotted with kids running pell-mell up and down with a kite attached to a ball of string.

An awful lot of time and effort went into perfecting our kites. Our fondest hope was to see our kite fly better than any other on the hill— to fly high and take our spirits soaring with it to undreamed-of heights, free and unbridled by the earthy restrictions placed upon human beings.

It must have been springtime extrasensory perception that drew us all to the hill on the first ideal kite-flying day. Our town didn't set aside an official kite day the way some communities did. Nevertheless, the competition was keen and

many shapes and sizes of kites appeared on the hill every year. Young and old alike were involved in kite making. The local grain elevator was swamped with kids begging wood for frames, and the grocers doled out yards of free string and wrapping paper.

People carefully guarded their cane fishing poles for fear they would end up as a frame for some kid's kite. Only the very rich or a most unimaginative child would dare buy a kite and run the risk of being snubbed by the do-it-yourself kite makers.

My spinster cousin, the local piano teacher, wrestled with kite building. She had a real fascination with kites and could be found on the hill struggling to get her kite airborne along with everyone else.

In those days, we girls didn't realize that kite flying was a sport for boys because we not only flew kites, but we built them, also.

I remember our first attempt at kite building. My sister and I enlisted the help of a master kite builder, my father. Things went well until the subject of a tail came up. Dad tried to tell us a tailless kite flew higher and straighter than one with a tail, but we insisted on adding a long, flowing, cumbersome tail made up of the most colorful rags we could find. Finally Dad threw up his hands in disgust and refused to give out any more advice.

Later, we carried our kite (with the gaudy tail) to the hill, and after several futile attempts to get it in the air, it was smashed beyond repair. Determined to have a kite that would fly, we hurried home, sneaked into the garage, and built a new one. Unwilling to admit Dad was right, when we returned to the hill, our beautiful tail was hidden under the seat of our Model-T Ford. We spent many happy carefree hours building and flying kites after the well-learned lesson that "Father knows best."

By the end of the day, the hillside resembled a battlefield. The wreckage of kites was strewn everywhere, dangling from trees, pieces floating in the ditch at the bottom of the hill and resting on rooftops. Anyone lucky enough to have his kite still afloat when his mother called him to supper anchored it to a tree or fence post and left it to dip and sway in the fading light in hopes of finding it still flying high the next day.

The kids, too, looked as though they had engaged the enemy in hand-to-hand combat. Aside from the runny noses which always seemed to go with kite flying, there were skinned knees and elbows, not to mention ripped, mud-caked clothes and wet footgear, gushing with every step as we trudged home, tired but happy. We must have been a hardy lot. None of us ever suffered any ill effects from the early outings.

Looking back, it is hard to believe that a thing as simple as a kite occupied so many of our minds for weeks at a time. Today, children have a cornucopia of toys from which to choose—an inexhaustible supply of recreational equipment and facilities to rely on for leisure activities. We were dependent on our own initiative to find suitable ways to spend our free time. Despite the lack of ready-made recreation, we were always busy, and idleness was unheard of.

I think one of the best pieces of wisdom I learned from nature was the value of the sheer joy and freedom of a windy spring day. I can't help but feel today's youngsters are being cheated out of a valuable part of their childhood. We grew up free from the pressures of modern times and blissfully ignorant of conditions as they exist in the world today. ❖

Forecast Weather Nature's Way

By Marilyn Pokorney

Today, with the flip of a dial, weather forecasts and warnings are at our fingertips. But before cable television, radar, weather satellites and other sophisticated electronic systems, people had to look to nature to predict the weather.

Most people—urban and rural alike—lived closer to nature than we do today. They depended on animals, insects, plants and other natural phenomena to predict weather changes.

Many people saw farm animals every day, so their behavior was the first to be noticed before weather conditions changed. Animals become more active when air pressure falls because they are uncomfortable. Cats and dogs become restless, ducks quack, hens squawk and cluster in groups, geese honk, donkeys bray, pigs squeal and roosters crow later in the day. Horses are nervous and young lambs, calves and foals play and frolic more than usual.

Most families owned cows. Even many townspeople owned at least one cow for milk, so cows became a popular weather prognosticator. It is said that cows bellow more before a shower. The more a cow swings her tail, the more severe an approaching storm will be, perhaps including hail.

According to farmers, pigs scratch their backs on fence posts when it's going to rain. Thermometers will rise if a pig digs a hole in the ground. And dogs and horses will sniff the air when rain is coming.

In humans as well as animals the senses of smell, hearing and sight all seem to heighten before a storm. In humid air, the horizon is crystal clear, the scent of flowers is much more pungent, and faraway sounds are easier to hear. Distant train whistles not usually heard are often an omen of rain.

Because wildlife was often trapped for food or pelts, people were familiar with how wild animals reacted to weather changes. Deer often leave high ground and come down to lower ground before stormy weather. Rabbits seek shelter before storms, so more rabbits were caught in traps when the weather was going to turn nasty.

Squirrels become quarrelsome and tend to be extra frisky before inclement weather. Female opossums and raccoons can be observed carrying their young from logs and dens to higher ground before a flooding rain.

If mice were in the house, people knew that when they heard more squeaking and scratching in the walls, bad weather was on the way.

Robins are known to sing more just before a rain. This was called "rain hollering." Because low air pressure makes it difficult to fly, birds fly erratically and lower than usual. Robins were commonly seen entering barns or sheds since birds seek shelter before unsettled weather.

Cowboys out on the range knew that when coyotes stayed close to their camps, a blizzard was soon to follow. Buzzards also mysteriously disappeared before a hailstorm.

A wind shift means a change of weather. Cowboys observed grass and leaves, as well as cattle, which would turn to face the wind.

Like birds, insects fly low in humid weather. This is advantageous to spiders and fish. Spiders normally spin webs between 6 and 7 p.m. They take their webs down early when it is going to rain. More insects are more easily caught. The spider reels in its catch before a heavy rain washes the web and prey away. Fish leap out of water and catch the lower-flying insects. For this reason, fishermen find that fish are harder to catch before a storm. The fish have already eaten and will not take bait.

Flies, gnats and fleas are especially troublesome before a storm. Even the lowly cockroach is more frolicsome before stormy weather. Insects of all kinds try to enter houses more frequently before unsettled weather. Ants build higher mounds to prevent rainwater from entering their nests. Some ants also close their holes. Butterflies cling to trees and the underside of leaves to protect their fragile wings from a forthcoming heavy rain.

When fireflies are out in large numbers, three days of nice weather can be expected.

By listening to insects, people could also judge temperatures. This was important because temperature rises before a storm. The higher the temperature, the closer bees stay to home. Bees stay in their hives at temperatures below 60 and above 102 degrees. Ants emerge from their nests when the temperature is 54 degrees or higher. Cicadas sing only in temperatures above 83 degrees.

Katydids shorten their calls at low temperatures. They are silent at 55 degrees. Locusts sing only when it is hot and dry. All insects are quiet if the temperature reaches 106 degrees.

Frogs were commonly used as weather forecasters, although the predictions varied. Some people said that frogs croak louder and longer before a rain, while others said that frogs croak more after a storm has passed.

Frogs were considered so reliable as weather indicators that they were captured and watched carefully, and in Europe a frog barometer was invented. A tree frog and miniature ladder were placed in a jar half-filled with water. If the frog remained in the water and croaked, the weather would be stormy. If the frog climbed the ladder and stayed there, the weather would turn clear and stay fair. This barometer is still used in some countries.

The Spanish invented a leech barometer. One or more leeches were placed in a jar with a little water. In good weather, the leech remained curled up at the bottom. Rain was expected if the leech crawled up to the top. If the leech swam rapidly, windy conditions were anticipated.

In 1851 a British scientist devised a leech barometer that was allegedly infallible. He placed a dozen leeches in a jar with a bell. If the bell remained quiet good weather was coming. If the leeches became active and rang the bell, stormy weather was on the way.

In the plant world, people look for various signs. Silver maples and cottonwoods magically turn silver before a rain. All deciduous trees turn the backs of their leaves 24 hours before wet weather. Some flower species close their blossoms before a rain; the daisy, morning glory, tulip and dandelion are common examples. Chickweed was known as the poor man's barometer because its leaves close when air pressure drops.

The sun, moon and sky were closely watched for changing weather conditions. Cirrus clouds, the light wispy ones, mean warm temperatures are coming. These clouds are referred to as "hen scratches." Altocumulus clouds mean rain is coming and are called "buttermilk sky" because of their curdlike appearance.

A pale moon or sun means rain is coming, as does a ring around either. A white moon with bright stars indicates fair weather, and in autumn, a frost. A red moon indicates rain. The Zuni Indians said, "A red moon has water in his eye."

Hippocrates, the Greek physician, taught that there was a relationship between disease and weather. Though people didn't understand why, most people noticed that when old wounds, surgical scars, bunions and arthritic joints hurt more than usual, it was going to storm. People with arthritis are sometimes called "human hygrometers." A hygrometer measures humidity, which apparently causes fluid in the joints and tissues to swell, making movement painful.

Cold, damp weather was known as "horse-chestnut weather." A New England superstition said if you carry a horse chestnut in your pocket, you won't get rheumatism.

While few people today rely on nature's way of predicting the weather, there is one indicator that still seems to hold a special fascination—the woolly bear caterpillar, the larva of the tiger moth.

It is said that the heavier the coat of this fuzzy caterpillar, the colder the winter will be. If there is a wide brown band between two black bands, the winter will be milder. But if it has no brown band the winter will be severe.

Some scientists have studied the predictions of the tiger moth larvae and have found them to be fairly accurate. Even today, while most people depend on radio and television forecasters, an astute observer of nature can sometimes predict the weather as accurately as meteorologists who have an arsenal of the latest scientific equipment at their disposal. ❖

points and hide scrapers. I found berry mashers, too and, on rare occasions, even discovered buffalo skulls.

The burgeoning of spring brought with it another blessed event—our Easter break from school. When I was a kid, we got two weeks. The only drawback was that before the holiday, we had to write Easter exams.

I didn't mind, though. The arrival of spring was so welcome that its coming actually sparked in me a renewed enthusiasm for schoolwork. My assignments got done on time, my attention span in class increased, and the grades I achieved on Easter exams were always the highest of the year. On more than one occasion, only this sporadic improvement kept me from having to repeat a term; all because I harbored a passionate anticipation for spring.

My time off from school wasn't all beer and skittles, however. Living on the farm meant doing chores every day. With the arrival of warm weather, I was also dragooned into helping Mom with spring cleaning. This was an annual event, and everyone in the family was expected to lend a hand.

For at least a week the household was in turmoil. The first job to be tackled was cleaning the stovepipes. After the fires in the basement furnace and kitchen range had

cooled, all the pipes were taken down, cleared of soot and reassembled. It was a dirty job and just the first of many.

All the walls, floors and ceilings had to be scrubbed. Invariably Mom decided that one room or another required a fresh look, if not with paint, then with wallpaper.

Even then we weren't finished. Rugs had to be beaten, bedding had to be aired, summer clothing had to be removed from storage trunks and winter things laid away in mothballs. When we finished, though, the spring break again became mine to enjoy, at least until it was time to return to classes.

Going back to school after Easter was a chore, but the drudgery was tempered by the knowledge that spring had come to stay. Watching the prairie transform itself day by day further dulled the sting.

In those days bountiful rains arrived on cue. Under their caress the landscape changed dramatically in a short time. They literally brought the countryside to life and portents of spring rapidly gave way to signs of impending summer.

As the days grew longer and the sun generated more warmth, vivid shades of green cloaked the land. Soon my youthful joy at the passing of winter was supplanted by an equally eager anticipation for the dog days of August. ❖

The Day Buck Creek Rose

By Hazel Humphers

Mama watched from the kitchen window of our weathered farmhouse as my older sisters Oma, Rubye and I skipped across the rocks that gave us dry passage of Buck Creek.

We were on our way to the one-room schoolhouse a mile over the hill on a May morning in 1920. I had coaxed Mama into letting me visit school with my sisters to celebrate my fifth birthday.

While she climbed the steep creek bank, Rubye asked Oma, "How wide is Buck Creek?"

Oma looked pleased to be asked such a grown-up question, and replied, "Papa says Buck Creek is about 60 feet wide and plenty deep." She spoke with the superiority that a third-grader might feel over a younger sister in her primer year.

When we reached the hilltop, we could see the frame schoolhouse, nestled in the valley near the railroad tracks. One train, the Katy passed each morning during 10 o'clock recess.

Papa headed for the barn. Soon he returned leading one of our workhorses, Old Charley. A roan, his dark red hair was splotched with white, and he had a white tail and mane.

"Oh, we must hurry!" Oma exclaimed. "There's our teacher!" Miss Reda stood in the schoolhouse doorway, wearing her stylish paisley dress. She rang the tardy bell.

At recess, while we watched the passenger train as it huffed and puffed around the bend, I noticed that Miss Reda watched the ominous clouds build in the western sky.

Back in the classroom she explained to the pupils, "You will need to eat your lunch here today. The rain clouds look bad. If they worsen, I will want all of you to go home early." She looked at me. "Hazel, your mother's note says for me to send you home right after recess. Thank you for visiting us on your birthday."

When I got home Mama and Papa were watching the clouds from our farmhouse kitchen door. Papa had come in from the field where he had been plowing. He said, "There's a big black cloud in the west. Looks like we might get a real gully-washer." As he spoke, the rain began to fall. Before Mama could answer, Papa continued, "Yes sir, it looks like it might rain the bottom out."

Mama began to worry about Oma and Rubye. As the rain fell in torrents her voice became anxious. "The good Lord has left the floodgates open again; we're having another flood."

"No," Papa mused, "it's just this part of the country, but it sure is coming down."

Suddenly, we heard a roar like a loud rumble of thunder. A swift deluge of water rushed down Buck Creek, overflowing its banks. The downpour persisted for a short time, and then, just as suddenly, subsided.

Mama wrung her hands and cried, "How will the girls get across the creek? They can't swim. Besides, the water is too swift. What will they do when they see the water is over the creek banks?"

I could tell Papa was thinking. I looked toward the schoolhouse and cried out, "Papa, there are Oma and Rubye on the other side of the creek."

Papa called to them. His soothing voice echoed through the hills. "Wait right there, girls, I'm coming after you."

Papa headed for the barn. Soon he returned leading one of our workhorses, Old Charley. A roan, his dark red hair was splotched with white, and he had a white tail and mane. Papa bridled him. We didn't have a saddle, so he got on Charley bareback. He asked Mama to get a rope to tie around his waist for the girls to hold onto. He would ride Charley while Charley swam across the creek for the girls.

Mama started crying and wringing her hands again. She asked, "Can Charley swim?"

Papa just looked at her and said, "All horses can swim." But I wondered if Papa could get Charley to enter the deep water.

What if he balked?

I heard Papa holler, "Giddy-up!" I closed my eyes for a moment. When I opened them, Charley was halfway across the creek, snorting water as he swam. Papa was still on Charley's back, holding on to the bridle, his legs hanging in the water.

When they reached the opposite creek bank, Rubye went first since she was youngest. She climbed onto Charley behind Papa, held onto the rope, and they brought her across. Mama seemed afraid to look, but they made it safely. Then Papa and Charley returned for Oma.

With everyone safe on the bank, Mama hugged Oma and Rubye. They were soaking wet. Wanting some attention, I pulled on Mama's dress tail and said, "Mama, maybe we could put the girls in the cookstove oven and dry them out like you do the wet chickens when it rains on them." Mama just looked at me and kept on hugging Oma and Rubye.

Papa unbridled Charley, but Charley waited on the creek bank, his eyes bright with pride. He seemed proud as punch of his heroic deed and looked as though he was ready to do it again. Papa motioned for him to go on.

Charley headed for the back side of the pasture in a gallop. His white tail swished in the cool evening breeze as he showed off to the mares. Surely they must have watched all the goings-on.

I leaned against Papa's leg. His wet pants smelled like catfish. He patted me on the head while Mama held onto Oma and Rubye and thanked God for Old Charley, and for God's help in our time of need. ❖

Tornado in the '20s

By Ona Webb Kettelkamp

Near noon on a rainy day in March, as I was seated in a little white church in the small town of Plainfield, near Joliet, Ill., an usher walked up the aisle and handed a written note to the pastor. The pastor paused in his sermon, took the message, glanced at it and read it aloud, "Five Corners has been wiped off the map by a tornado."

Everyone was aware that the Webb residence was located one farm east of Five Corners. Mother at the organ, Father in the choir, my brother, our neighbor Mrs. Stice, and I arose together and left the sanctuary. Others followed. My brother rushed out into

The Webb farm home before the tornado of 1920.

the drenching rain to our large seven-passenger Reo car parked in front of the church. We attempted to follow him, but the torrents of rain held us back for a few minutes.

We could only cover four of the five miles to Five Corners. Debris was strewn over the road. Electric and trolley-line wires hung over the highway. My brother ran our car into a side ditch. As we jumped out we could hear voices warning, "Watch out for the wires!" The two menfolk ran ahead, picking their way through the tangle of fallen limbs and lumber. We followed more slowly, praying aloud as we threaded our way in and out of the rubble.

My brother Russell returned to tell us that all of our relatives were safe, but that we should be careful as we walked home. Our neighbor, Mrs. Stice, had left her husband and 6-month-old baby home while she went to church with us. Their place was beyond ours. Her husband and

baby had to be helped out of their damaged home. He was standing on the lower steps of the basement stairs holding the baby in his arms, trying to decide whether he should step into the flooded basement for safety.

Our home was a new house on the north side of the street across from the farm place. The street was the Lincoln Highway, between Joliet and Aurora. My older sister and my brother's wife and 3-year-old son were safe in our home. They had attended Sunday school and returned home on the streetcar. My sister had called my sister-in-law about 10 minutes after they arrived home and asked her to come over for dinner. She replied that she would have to wait until the rain let up a bit more.

In a few minutes she, her son and little dog walked across the street to our house. She was carrying a kettle of peeled potatoes and her little boy. They had trouble getting in through the side door because of the heavy winds and pouring rain. Both women tried to close the door, but it was swollen from the heavy rains. Also, they had to replace the heavy brace they had earlier braced against the door. This frightened them, and they immediately went to the windward side of the basement and stayed there.

The little dog who followed my sister-in-law had run back across the street. They found him later, next to the barn door, killed. Evidently that was as far as he could get before the tornado struck.

Through the basement windows the women could see telephone poles and trolleys swaying.

Automobiles ran into ditches. The men drove their cars into ditches because it was safer and gave more protection from the wind. My sister-in-law could hear the terrific roar of the tornado, but my sister was deafened for several hours.

As calm came over the place, the women ventured up to the first floor. When they reached it everything seemed dark, so they went back to the basement windows. Finally, they went upstairs again. The front and side windows were matted with wet straw and hay. The women managed to find a peephole in the front hall window toward the street. Through it they could see that all the farm buildings were gone and that the house was badly damaged.

Our neighbor whose place was two farms east of ours, and located on a hill, stood transfixed at a window, watching the funnel-shaped cloud swoop down and strike our place. His wife could not pull him away from the window. He said, "We're safe. It's taking the Webb place and striking Five Corners."

The two places at Five Corners, where five roads meet, were laid flat. One man was killed. He was found clinging to the outside pump, apparently killed instantly. His wife, pinned in the basement under fallen timbers, suffered several broken bones.

Our buildings except for the house were swept from the ground, and some were blown miles away. Big timbers were embedded deep into the ground. Our farm buildings were rebuilt later with other farmers' lumber and our lumber helped rebuild other buildings farther away.

The big pitchfork from the hayloft was found hanging in the bay window of the farmhouse. The kitchen had collapsed. It was weird; all the pictures and dishes were broken, but on one wall in an adjoining room, a mirror still hung not only intact, but in perfect balance.

Men worked late into the night rounding up livestock. Cattle and horses ran wild for some time. Fences were destroyed. Rescuing our

The Webb farm home after the tornado.

young horses was quite a feat. The wet, matted straw and hay fell down from the loft and weighted down the horses in the stalls were they were tied. My brother stood with one foot on one horse's back and the other foot on another horse's back as the men worked to remove the heavy, wet straw. He tried to calm the horses. Naturally, they were very excited.

Later in the afternoon of the day of the tornado, all of Joliet seemed to come to see the stricken area. The Catholic priest from Joliet was among the first to reach our place that afternoon.

Part of our new home's roof had been blown off, but our old home place could not be lived in without considerable repair. Our lawns were covered with debris.

But before we realized it, people were pouring into the house, even tearing pieces of woodwork off for souvenirs. I was asked to stay at one of the doors of the damaged house to keep people from entering. One young man came to the door. I told him we were keeping people from entering. He said, "Don't you know me? I'm your cousin and I came down from Chicago as soon as I heard about the tornado. I'm here to help."

On the morning after the tornado we began to make bread and cook food in order to have plenty for the workers on the following days. There was no need for this preparation, because plenty of food was brought in by neighbors and friends.

Many pictures were taken of the stricken area and given to us by our friends. We never thought of taking pictures. One of the snaps of my father shows that he has one kind of shoe on one foot and a different kind on the other.

We learned a lot about true friendship at such times. Our buildings were rebuilt and fields cleared by our many friends. What we would have done without all those wonderful people I will never know. ❖

Bobby, the Twister Hero

By Ruth Byrd

In the early 1940s, we were tenant farmers for a prominent businessman, C.C. Cranford. He owned a large farm. He had 50 or more white-faced cattle, and he raised a lot of hogs and chickens to sell.

It was my father and brothers' job to do the farming and take care of the cows and hogs. My mother, the other children and I took care of the chickens and our own animals.

Our house sat up on a high hill and was half surrounded by big old oak trees. At the foot of this hill was a bottom, and on the far side of the bottom was a river that overflowed quite often and flooded this bottom and also some others on the farm. The bottom near the house had a big tree in the middle. Once when the river flooded, my brothers got in a boat and rowed up under this tree. The lowest limb was about 10 feet high, and they rowed the boat under this limb, climbed out the limb and up the tree. Quite often fish were found in ditches after the water had run down.

Now to the tornado. Mr. Cranford had a long chicken house and also a machine house, each 30 by 100 feet long. Both sat up on pillars. We kept our animals in an old barn with a shingle roof. The roof needed repair, but I guess it was just as well the men didn't get around to fixing it. All these buildings sat out in the open.

One day, late in the evening, the air became still and the sky turned a whitish yellow color. I was about 17 years old, a girl, but still I had to split the wood for the cookstove and get it when the boys were in the field and didn't have time. I was just finishing when suddenly the wind started blowing. All the family was scattered here and there, doing their regular chores. A hired hand was driving a tractor home from the fields. My mother was coming in from doing the milking.

My father and my youngest brother's collie dog, Bobby, were over near the big new barn, driving up the white-faced cows. For some reason, Bobby wanted to act ugly and wouldn't let the cows go near the barn. Daddy got very mad at him, but in a matter of minutes, he knew why Bobby was acting so strangely. A tornado was close by.

When it hit, it took some of the tin off the big barn roof, blew across the bottoms and took the old shingle roof off the old barn—just raised it as if you'd picked it up—and sat it down over the pasture. It blew the machine and chicken houses partially off their pillars and caused an old corn picker to almost run over my mother.

I was so frightened that I ran inside the house and out again. Big trees were falling, so I was afraid to stay outside, but I was afraid to stay in the house, too.

The hired hand could hardly control the tractor. The wind blew his hat off and he never saw it again. Later we found pieces of the shiny tin barn roof over in the woods a good half-mile away.

All the while, our nearest neighbors sat on their front porch and watched. It missed their house by a matter of yards. They didn't even feel it.

After it was all over, Dad realized why Bobby made the cows stay on the lower ground. He knew the tornado was coming, but Dad didn't. Through some inner instinct Bobby protected our herd, and that made him a hero. Mr. Cranford loved him and offered Daddy $150 for him. That was right much money at the time, but Daddy wouldn't accept it. Bobby belonged to my 4-year-old brother and was his pet.

We still go back to the old place once in awhile, but things have really changed. Most of the buildings are gone, but the clubhouse remains. The river seldom floods anymore since a dam has been built several miles up the river, and the old farm has been made into a golf course now. It is very nice, but it will never mean as much to me as it did when I was a girl growing up. ❖

Aunt Blanche's Old Storm Cellar

By Loula Dickerson Arnold

*I*t's strange how a small incident will bring to memory another event we thought we had forgotten. Childhood memories are supposedly the most vivid after reaching our middle years. Even so, it is sometimes surprising to recall something we had not thought about for many years.

Such was my experience recently when I was awakened by a gust of wind, followed by loud, shaking thunder. The black clouds hanging off to the west reminded me of similar nights more than 75 years ago, when I was a very small child living with my parents on the plains of western Kansas.

Every spring, my sister, Wilma Jane, and I looked forward to going to Uncle Hank's and Aunt Blanche's to spend our summer vacation. We left just as soon as school was out, and although they only lived about 30 miles from us, it was a long trip in those days. We felt like we were far, far from home.

Their only child was a boy, and perhaps that's why it seemed that our aunt and uncle regarded us more as daughters than nieces. They always tried to make our visits very pleasant.

I remember many things that happened during those summers. But my most vivid memories are of those times when Aunt Blanche would awaken in the middle of the night, frightened by the angry thunder clouds that so often hung over the barren, windswept prairie.

She usually woke our cousin, Charley, Wilma Jane and me with these words: "Get up and dress quickly, children. We must go to the

Seeing heavy, dark clouds forming overhead, she beckoned to Charley, Wilma Jane and me, and we hurried for the cellar.

cellar, for there is going to be a terrible storm and I want to get you all down where it is safe."

I also remember how peaceful my uncle looked at that crucial moment, still lying there in his bed in untroubled slumber. Sometimes I'd ask, "Are we going to let Uncle Hank stay up here in the house and blow away all by himself?"

Aunt Blanche usually replied, "I finally got him awake and warned him that a big storm was brewing, and he is just too contrary to get up and get himself to safety." My aunt was excellent when it came to paraphrases and quotations, and she always ended her sentences at a time like that with, "The good Lord helps those who help themselves."

The cellar was always damp and cold. We three youngsters all huddled beside Aunt Blanche, grinding our teeth to keep them from chattering. Auntie was always reassuring, though, and tried to keep up a lively conversation, even when the water started running in on the floor up to our ankles. I'd sit there and long for the nice, warm feather bed I had just left, and think of Uncle Hank in his warmth and comfort. But never once did I ever say that to my aunt. I felt that I should be loyal to her; after all, wasn't she thinking solely of our safety?

Charley sometimes ridiculed her as we opened the door and crawled out of the cellar. "See, Mom?" he'd say. "Nothin' happened. It never does—and I'm frozen to death!" But both Wilma Jane and I always showed disappointment that the house was still standing on its foundation, trying to make Aunt Blanche understand that we appreciated her interest in our welfare.

I'll never forget how calm and well rested Uncle Hank looked one morning, sitting there by the fire, drinking a steaming cup of coffee, when we came in through the back door at the break of day after having spent several hours in the storm cellar. Looking at our muddy feet, wet clothing and dripping hair, he said, "Once I saw an old wet cat and three half-drowned kittens that looked better than you all do this morning." There's no need to quote Aunt Blanche's response.

As I recall the frightening storm clouds during my childhood, I also remember the day Aunt Blanche promised to do some baking for her Women's Missionary Society. She had just removed a huge chocolate cake from the oven when she heard the first echoes of thunder. Seeing heavy, dark clouds forming overhead, she beckoned to Charley, Wilma Jane and me, and we hurried for the cellar. A couple of hours later, we removed our shoes, waded out and made for the kitchen door.

Aunt Blanche was the first to enter, and she let out an awful moan. I was right behind her, and as I reached to lend her support, I wondered if a big bolt of lightning had killed my wonderful uncle. Uncle Hank wasn't dead, but I'm sure my aunt could have choked him to death with great pleasure, for there before her sat my uncle, calmly eating a giant slice of Aunt Blanche's cake. As we stumbled in, he looked up, placid and serene, and inquired, "Did it rain much down where you came from?"

Ignoring that remark, my aunt moaned, "Oh, Hank, my lovely cake! I baked it for the Missionary Society. What will I do now? How could you? Oh, how could you?"

"Easy," growled Uncle Hank. "I just used a knife. You can just tell 'em you had to go to that underground retreat of yours right at suppertime and that I got hungry." Then, grinning, Uncle Hank put on his old hat and reached for the milking pail.

This remarkable couple lived out their twilight years on the old homestead where Uncle Hank had brought his bride shortly after the turn of the century. As long as she lived, every time Aunt Blanche saw a cloud as big as Uncle Hank's hat, she would go to the cellar. But she never was able to coax my uncle into going with her. There just never was a western tornado cloud big enough to make Uncle Hank leave a nice warm bed in the middle of the night to accompany Aunt Blanche to the cellar.

Last summer I visited the haunts of my childhood. The big red barn, the white house, the old windmill and even the fruit orchard were gone from the farm. Only the old storm cellar remained, evidence that at one time, a pioneering family had lived on that plot of ground. Evidence that babies were born and that one man and his wife tilled the ground, raised a family on its good soil, and loved it. ❖

Old-Timer's Weather Forecast

By Marie Marshall

When restless winds begin to blow
and darkened clouds are hanging low,
When smoke comes down and puppies sleep
and frogs from under lilies peep,
When the sun is pale as it goes down
and the moon wears halos for a crown,
When chairs and tables start to groan
and Grandma's joints cause her to moan,
When hens cluck loud and the kittens mew
and walls are damp as morning dew,

When humid air causes hogs to snort
and flies annoy the cows for sport,
When the cricket's chirp is high and clear
and the fawn crowds close to mother deer,
When fish in the pond begin to rise
and squalid toads blink sleepy eyes,
When a fox eats grass on yonder hill
and the blackbird's call is sharp and shrill,
When swallows perch on a weather vane,
you can be sure it's gonna rain. ❖

How to Foretell the Weather

A barometer provides the best method of forecasting the weather.

By Anna Carman

These instructions are from Ballard's Blue Book of Information for All the Family for a barometer that used to hang on our kitchen cabinet door in the 1930s and 1940s.

Rapid rise—unsettled weather
Gradual rise—settled weather
Rise in cold, dry air in summer— wind from north
Rise in moist air and low temperature— wind and rain from north
Rise with winds from south— fine weather
No change with dry air— continued fine weather
Rapid fall—stormy weather
Rapid fall with west wind— storm from north
Fall with north wind— storm with rain or snow
Fall with moist air and rising temperature— rain from south
Fall with dry air and falling temperature in winter—snow

Even if you have no barometer, you can still forecast the weather for many hours ahead with fair accuracy:

A red sunset, slightly purple, with bright blue sky overhead foretells fine weather.

A gray, cloudy sunset indicates rain. If the sun looks indistinct and white before sunset, it foretells storms.

A whitish yellow sunset sky means rain during the night or early the next day.

Brilliant and queer colors in the sunset, with hard outlines around the clouds, foretell rain and probably wind.

Usually clear air and very bright stars are an indication of rain.

A red sky in the morning means much wind and rain. A gray sky in the morning with breaking clouds indicates fine weather.

Fogs foretell settled weather.

If distant sounds carry very distinctly, rain will come soon.

Heavy dew in hot weather means continued fine weather. No dew foretells rain.

Changeable winds are an indication of changeable weather.

If the clouds move in a different direction from the air on the ground, the wind is changing.

Soft, delicate-looking clouds are an omen of fine weather.

Hard-edged, oily looking clouds mean wind.

Small, inky clouds foretell rain.

Small clouds driven across heavy, massive clouds mean wind and rain.

Clouds like streamers, moving rapidly and high in the air, foretell an approaching storm.

A morning rainbow means rain; an evening rainbow, fair weather.

The moon has absolutely no connection with the weather. ❖

Recycling Fans & Hot Summers

By Marjorie Barton

When part of our country experiences heat with record-breaking temperatures, I am always reminded of hot summers long ago and faraway. We may not have known we were poor, but we knew it was hot.

One of the facts my high-school teacher Miss Billings impressed on me is that everything happens in cycles. I'm not sure why that tidbit of truth fascinated me, but it did. Although I suppose she was referring to depressions and wars and prosperity and peace, she also made references to heat and cold waves.

If you have never lived where the temperature is consistently 100-plus with 95-percent humidity, you are lucky. During my last years as an educator in West Texas, we were greeted with August temperatures of 100, 113 and 117° F. About that time, I said, "Enough!" I vowed to live in the state of Washington, regardless of my income.

How did we keep cool? With a 10-inch electric fan! It helped— if you remained very still. The best way to stay still was by listening to Ma Perkins and other exciting radio soap operas.

But I remember hotter summers than those. My mother made the rules during the 1930s—the hot, dry summers of the Dust Bowl era. We were in Okmulgee, Okla., and she decided it was not warm enough to swim unless the temperature had been at least 90 degrees for a week.

One summer the temperatures were recorded at 118 and 121° F (in the shade)—Death Valley temperatures, they said. (Mother said no one would believe her later if she said that, so she saved the newspaper clippings.)

How did we keep cool? With a 10-inch electric fan! It helped—if you remained very still. The best way to stay still was by listening to Ma Perkins and other exciting radio soap operas.

Mother sometimes let me indulge in a little of Bob Wills and His Texas Playboys. I'll never forget Ida Reed and *Take Me Back to Tulsa, I'm Too Young to Marry.*

While we listened to the radio, the tiny fan stirred hot air around the room. How distinctly I remember the height of that heat wave! When we came out of church on Sunday, a big thermometer in a storefront registered more than 110°—and it was only noon. Daddy bought a block of ice and we took it home, put it in a dishpan and let the fan blow across it.

More impressive than the little fan at home were the big black ceiling fans in the downtown stores and our Baptist church. I can hear the whir of those fans to this day.

Equally fascinating were the small hand-held fans, provided in the songbook racks along with the hymnals. The pictures on those fans provided a brief diversion for bored—but very quiet—little people.

Playtime was decidedly better outside the hot house. When the porch was shaded, that was the best place. Once I noticed the thermometer was on the shady side of the porch pedestal. I was 6 at the time and had been taught how to read the thermometer. I could not understand why my mother put the thermometer in the shade if she expected to know how hot it was. I moved the thermometer into the sun and watched the mercury rise. Then I returned it to the shade and went about my play. I did this several times, unaware that the thermometer often broke because of the extreme heat in the sun.

Once Mother caught me. She was angry, but she knew that I did not understand the consequences of putting a thermometer in the sun. I didn't do it anymore!

By nightfall, the inside of the house was unbearable. Many people put cots or quilts in their backyards in order to get any rest at all, and that's what we did. This also afforded us a chance for an astronomy lesson. We learned about the Milky Way, the Big and Little Dippers and other constellations. We also watched for falling stars. Thus, those hot, uncomfortable nights turned into pleasant experiences until the mosquitoes forced us back inside.

Cycles come and go, hot and cold; fans come and go and return; stars are remembered; radio came, faded and has returned with gusto.

Now, just as then, we listen to the radio, watch the stars, use a fan. I suppose it is all part of a cycle. I like it! ❖

Equally fascinating were the small hand-held fans, provided in the songbook racks along with the hymnals. The pictures on those fans provided a brief diversion for bored—but very quiet—little people.

Dust Bowl Days

By Grover Brinkman

*D*o the words "Dust Bowl" have any meaning for you? What about the word "Okie"? They are reminders of one of the worst prolonged droughts the nation has ever experienced. It spread over a half-dozen states.

If you're a senior citizen, you well remember the Dust Bowl days. If you're much younger, you've read about it, or perhaps you've seen a rerun of the old movie *The Grapes of Wrath* with Henry Fonda. Those were horrendous days that will always have a place in our history books.

A series of prolonged droughts over mid-America turned millions of cultivated acres into desert. The states most affected were Oklahoma, Texas, Kansas, Nebraska and the Dakotas. As the drought lengthened, the dry, powdery topsoil was picked up by prevailing winds and carried for hundreds of miles. Crops withered, streams dried up, wells gave out. Dust from Oklahoma and Texas was seen in the red-brown skies that dimmed the sun in southern Illinois.

In the stricken areas, cattle died by the thousands. Some ranchers even shot their animals to put them out of their misery. Poverty stalked the land. The words "Dust Bowl" dominated the newspaper headlines. One could travel for a hundred miles through Oklahoma, Texas or Kansas without seeing a blade of green. People by the hundreds left the stricken land, heaping their belongings on any vehicle they owned, and headed down Route 66 for California. Thus was born the word "Okie."

Life magazine sent Margaret Bourke White and other top photographers and reporters to the stricken areas, and they produced awesome photos of ranch houses half-buried by the dust; of cattle so emaciated their ribs showed through their hides; of people on the march, mothers afoot with babies in their arms; and of the stricken land.

Man did not cause the droughts, of course. But man was responsible for the dust storms that followed. Greedy, he plowed up each tillable acre.

> **The words "Dust Bowl" dominated the newspaper headlines. One could travel for a hundred miles through Oklahoma, Texas or Kansas without seeing a blade of green.**

He forgot about trees and their worth, and chopped them down to produce more cropland. He destroyed the natural cover of the land, and when the drought set in, the land simply blew away. Topsoil turned into powdery dust, and the wind did the rest.

The condition of the land called for drastic government action. The first remedy took place at the farm of M.E. Curtis near Magnum, Okla. A tiny ponderosa pine tree was planted in the dust, and watered so that it would take root. It was the first of millions of trees planted in the Dust Bowl as shelterbelts. Politicians scoffed. But they were powerless to stop the movement initiated by President Franklin Delano Roosevelt when he asked the U.S. Forest Service for an estimate for a shelterbelt of trees that would stretch from Texas to Nebraska.

His critics laughed at the idea. But Roosevelt was adamant. Long before the dust storms worsened, he had discussed the idea with Henry Wallace, then secretary of agriculture. Roosevelt believed that a canopy of trees induced rainfall, and he knew that they offered the land protection.

Despite the critics, the tree-planting program was soon underway. Soon 5½ million young trees had been planted.

The drought continued into the following year, but the tree planting never slowed. By the end of the following autumn, there were 18 million young trees growing. Five years later, more than 40 million seedlings had taken root.

This was slow, discouraging work. Immediate results could not be evaluated. But the work went on regardless. Eight years later, the U.S. Forest Service had planted 200 million trees and shrubs as shelterbelts. The foresters were faced with many problems: soil, drought, wind velocity and erosion. Many types of trees were used in the experiment. Of course, some of them died. But an estimated 60 percent grew.

Today, those seedlings are tall trees, doing their duty in soil conservation. This vast experiment of rebirth in a denuded land has taught Americans a vital lesson: Conservation must be observed in all forms of agriculture. If a tree is cut, it must be replaced. It's as simple as that.

We still have droughts, but we no longer have bulbous dust storms that darken the sky. The tons and tons of topsoil are gone forever. Man's greed was a very expensive lesson. But a little ponderosa pine answered the critics. Old-timers remember the dust storms of yesterday very poignantly; the young can read the true impact in their history books. ❖

The Magic of Rainmakers in Kansas

By Estelle C. Laughlin

It was the Fourth of July! There was a celebration at the big grove six miles distant, but it might as well have been 600 miles, for our family wasn't going. The wind hadn't blown for four days!

The water tanks were down to the green moss in the bottom. Father and the hired man were stationed at the pump, pumping while the thirsty cattle bellowed as they gathered at the pasture gate, trying to get to the tanks. We children looked up reproachfully at the big Dempster windmill on the hill and at the Eclipse mill towering above the milk house and tank. We looked up at the heavens. Why didn't it rain?

That night at the supper table, our father told the hired man about a spell back in 1890 in Kansas when it didn't rain for weeks and weeks and the crops shriveled in the heat. "Pluviculture," as rainmakers called their work, became quite popular during those arid years, and the rainmakers went abroad in the land. Their work continued for several years until even the government scientists gave up on the notion that rain could be produced by artificial means and at the will of the operator.

It was frequently said that the rainmaking episode in Kansas was the most costly fraud ever perpetrated upon the people of the state.

Several individuals who called themselves "professors" professed to have formula for making rain. They traveled all over Kansas and collected many thousands of dollars from farmers and businessmen.

Father said that most Kansans laugh about the rainmakers now, although some of them do so a bit sheepishly. But, it wasn't a laughing matter in the beginning; even the government spent thousands of dollars on the idea, and a corporation backed by practical Eastern financiers, the Rock Island Railroad, also put some of its money into a project of this type.

The idea of making rain artificially developed during the Civil War. Soldiers were impressed by the terrific rains that drenched battlefields directly after battles in which cannon played a prominent part. They reasoned that the cannonading created disturbances in the atmosphere that produced precipitation. In a state settled by veterans, it was natural that people should believe that bombarding the skies would compel the clouds to disgorge some of their water.

The Rock Island Railroad had just finished its line into Dodge City when one of the most severe droughts of the time occurred. Delegations of farmers called on Rock Island officials and pointed out that "Providence couldn't produce any rain; how about the railroads trying?" The railroad officials put their chemists to work to see what they could develop. All along the Rock Island lines west of Hutchinson, the company placed advertisements in the newspapers that its own "rainmaking machine" would be at Dodge City.

On the appointed day, farmers gathered from miles around. They came in buckboards and on horseback, some from Oklahoma, Colorado and farther north to witness firsthand this tampering with the elements. Many traveled for two days or more to get to Dodge City for the big show.

Shortly before noon, a special train pulled in bearing the rainmaking contraption on a flatcar. The apparatus was described as a monster mortar, "a sort of cross between a cannon of exceptionally large caliber and a giant slingshot."

The workmen spent hours preparing the equipment for the demonstration. Thousands of people milled around the car, asking questions and offering advice. When the contraption finally was ready, an official of the railroad company quieted the crowd. He said that no one knew whether the apparatus would produce results. He pointed out that the company had the interests of the people at heart and was willing to spend its own money in an effort to produce rain for the district's crops.

Chemical bombs were placed in the cannon and thrown into the air by the slingshot. A dozen or more bombs were discharged, emitting a cloud of yellowish smoke. The crowd was satisfied with the demonstration and started homeward, expecting to be drenched by a downpour. But nothing happened!

On July 15, 1891, the United States Department of Agriculture sent its own crew of rainmakers into western Kansas. The crew had three different types of equipment to demonstrate. One was a set of wooden mortars that hurled chemical bombs into the air. These bombs exploded at a height of 600–800 feet. The second line of offense against the recalcitrant raindrops was a barrage of 60 balloons, each 10

feet in diameter, filled with oxygen and hydrogen gas. The balloons were connected with the ground by wire so they could be exploded electrically at the proper height.

Next came 100 kites, each five feet tall; each wore a long tail at the end of which was a dynamite bomb. The kites were also connected to the ground by wires so that the bombs could be exploded by an electrical charge.

Thousands of people made long trips to observe this demonstration. The records do not disclose that any rain fell soon afterward.

The outfit was then taken to what was known as the Staked Plains area, now the Panhandle region of Texas. More balloons and more kites were sent aloft and their charges were exploded. The local newspapers reported that a 5-inch rain, starting the night of the demonstration and continuing all the next day, soaked the parched earth and gave great encouragement to the rainmakers.

The first of the rainmaking corporations organized in Kansas was the Interstate Artificial Rain Co., with $50,000 in capital. It had a contract to produce rain at Atwood, in northwest Kansas, but the demonstration failed. The Swisher Rain Co. was organized with capital of $100,000. The Goodland Artificial Rain Co. was probably the last of the rainmaking corporations in Kansas. It had a capital of $50,000.

Pluviculture became quite an industry in the Midwest. In addition to the corporations, several individuals who called themselves "professors" professed to have formula for making rain. They traveled all over Kansas and collected many thousands of dollars from farmers and businessmen. My father told of contributing to an itinerant professor who guaranteed to produce an inch of rain in central Nebraska.

Above: In 1956 The Rainmaker, *starring Burt Lancaster and Katherine Hepburn, was filmed. Lancaster played Bill Starbuck, a rainmaker come to the plains to put an end to the drought. Facing page: Burt is pictured in his rainmaker garb.*

It was customary for the professor to set up a shack on the top of a hill. Two ordinary smokestacks made from common stovepipe cut through the roof of this "laboratory." The "scientist" would not allow anyone in the shack while he was mixing his chemicals. After some young fellows in the neighborhood rode their ponies up to the shack for a closer look, they reported that they could not see any smoke coming from the chimneys, or any other signs of chemical activity. However, that night it rained, and the "professor" collected his money from all the farmers in that neighborhood before moving on to other dry spots.

One of these professors went to South Dakota and agreed to produce at least a half-inch of rain within 48 hours. The farmers collected $500 cash and deposited it with a banker. When more than an inch of rain fell the next day, the professor was paid and hailed as the savior of their crops. Some of the hardheaded farmers got together and decided it would be a good thing to have some of that chemical formula on hand all the time, and they began negotiating with the professor. He finally agreed to sell the formula for $15,000 to be used whenever needed in that section, on condition that his secret formula should never be made public. Several counties actually voted to issue bonds and turned them over to the rainmaker, who promptly sold the bonds and disappeared.

Chemists who later examined the "secret formula" found that it contained nothing that would cause rain. There were some sadder and wiser farmers in that locale after that.

Some of the itinerant professors traveled in wagons in which they carried their equipment. One rainmaker had his family traveling with him in a covered wagon. Somehow, the sight of those towheaded children and that weary wife gave the farmers additional confidence in the professor.

These professors traveled up and down western Kansas, Texas, Nebraska and the Dakotas. Wherever they could get a group of farmers to put up a little money, they would set up their outfits and go to work. Local showers were an ordinary occurrence along the streams in the drought area, even during dry periods, and it was later noticed that the professors always operated along the streams.

Although the idea of rainmaking has never been abandoned entirely, there have been no serious attempts to alter the elements by such primitive artificial means for many years. Like the dodo birds, the rainmakers just disappeared.

In the 1950s, new types of scientists used airplanes to "seed" the clouds in an effort to prevent disastrous hailstorms throughout the Midwest. The young farmers were greatly impressed; several seasons went by with the "cloud seeders" preventing severe hail damage to crops, or so it was believed. Then one such attempt to stop a hailstorm resulted in a cloudburst that washed out acres of cropland. The older men who remembered the rainmakers of the 1890s said, "I told you so." In one western Nebraska county, some of the older farmers even took legal action to prevent continued "cloud seeding." Many argued that cloud seeding was "going against God's will." (However, these same people had become accustomed to vaccination to prevent scourges of smallpox.)

Many people are satisfied merely to wait and see what develops. After all, with space stations in orbit and astronauts walking in space, why couldn't it be possible to make rain or prevent hailstorms? ❖

When rainmakers failed during droughts, folks on the plains— like their forebears for generations—turned to the Almighty for the life-giving water they so desperately needed.

© Jim Daly '80

Playing in the Rain

By Helen Colwell Oakley

*I*t's raining! It's raining! It's raining!" First one big, beautiful drop fell and then another and another—the first raindrops in months and months. My sisters, brothers and I were playing in the yard of our large country home in rural New York state. The year was in the early 1930s and I was 10 or 11. My sisters and brothers were all younger. The youngest was a baby boy named Joey.

We didn't need to be told twice to go out to play in the rain!

It was summertime, and all of us were gathered on the large front lawn, under the spreading maple trees, to catch a cool breeze if one should come our way. The radio announcer had forecast another day in the 90s.

All conversations began with a discussion of the weather. Grandpa said it was 20 degrees hotter; Gram said that we should do all heavy work in the forenoon before the temperature climbed; and the neighbor lady just kept fanning herself with a rolled-up newspaper while she sat in her rocker on the stoop. Our lawn wasn't soft and green and velvety as it usually was because it had been so dry. There had been no rain for several months.

Across the road was our large red barn. We watched as the hired men brought in huge loads of loose hay. Teams of horses pulled the hay riggings alongside of the barn. Then one team was unhitched so that they could be hooked onto the large hayfork. One man jumped onto the hayfork and then signaled to the man driving the team. "Giddap!" he hollered, and a big forkful of hay slowly swung up into the loft.

"Whoa!" yelled the man on the load. Then he jerked the rope, and down came the hay, into the mow. The men in the mow shook it out and spread it evenly.

The man unloading would take the horses back and forth across the barnyard until the fork had unloaded all the load; then the next load would be drawn into the barn and the team would unload it. This continued until all the riggings were empty. The horses were getting overheated; the men took off their denim work shirts, soaked with perspiration, and mopped their faces with their bright red and white bandanna handkerchiefs.

We children were perspiring on the lawn in the shade. It was that hot. We had had day after day of this hot, sticky weather, and we prayed for relief. The wells and springs were getting low and the crops were bad, the grown-ups said. Besides, we wanted it to rain so that we could play in the rain. This was our favorite delight.

But we waited for days, and still, no rain in sight! Some days, the radio announcer on the Atwater Kent radio said that we might get some rain soon, but most of the time he just said, "No rain in sight." Everything looked sad—so dry and parched and hanging over. Mom's roses didn't do so well, even though water was sprayed on them every evening. The sun was burning them to the high heavens, she said. Her roses were always so fabulously gorgeous, but not this year.

Usually the big farmhouse was comfortably cool at night for sleeping, but not this summer—it was too hot and sticky. The mornings didn't seem fresh and new anymore, either. "Leave off your undershirts, petticoats and socks for today," Mom said when she called us as we were getting dressed.

"Woweee!" we hollered. This was great; we were never allowed to go without our undershirts, petticoats and socks. We would catch our death of foolishness, Gram said. The baby was dressed in just his band and diaper. Imagine—no undershirt, kimono or booties! Babies were always dressed abundantly, even in warm weather, or they might get colic for sure.

Mom had the dark green window shades drawn as soon as the sun came over the mountain. She said it would help to keep the house cooler. All the blankets and spreads were stripped from the beds, and the beds were made up with just the clean, white sheets. I did not like the beds without fancy spreads on them; however, they did look cooler.

After we ate our shredded wheat and toast, we were sent out into the yard to play. Around noontime, my sister said, "Stop throwing water on my mud pies!" No one was throwing any water around that we could see, but then a drop fell on my arm, and then one fell on the baby's face. Sure enough, drops of rain were falling!

We all raced up onto the porch, excitedly shouting, "Mom, it's raining!"

Mom raced to the screen door to see what the commotion was all about. Then she spotted the large splotches on the sidewalk. All of us went out into the yard to feel the wonderful raindrops. Then Mom panicked— she had the baby diapers spread all over the backyard to bleach and dry in the noonday sun! So we all scurried to gather them up before they got soaked. Then she shooed her hens through the henhouse door, as she was afraid that we might get a bad storm. She thought a lot of her hens.

What fun! Our hair got wet, and soon, water was running off us like it does off a duck's back.

Mom said that we could go out to play in the rain—if we stayed close to the house, 'cause it might blow up a thunderstorm. We didn't need to be told twice to go out to play in the rain! We hurried upstairs to put on our bathing suits. They weren't skimpy, like they are today. We were bare just from the knees down, and on top, only our arms and a little shoulder were exposed. It had been so long since we had a chance to play in the rain that we could barely get changed, we were so excited.

Finally we raced down the steps two at a time. Sister Rose, who was 5, beat all of us down the stairs because she slid down the banister. She knew how to do it better than any of us. (My feet always seemed to tangle in the spindles.)

As we dashed through the door, Mom called, "You kids come right in if you hear any thunder or see any lightning, do you hear?" But there was no thunderstorm—just huge raindrops at first, and then a nice, gentle rain. What fun! Our hair got wet, and soon, water was running off us like it does off a duck's back.

Speaking of ducks, Mom's ducks, a drake and the little ducklings came around the porch and headed straight for the puddle that was forming below the eaves troughs. They quacked and shook their feathers in delight. The horses were out in the pasture, too, rolling and kicking on the wet grass, thoroughly enjoying their rainy romp.

The hired men were sopping wet from putting canvases on two loads of hay that they couldn't get into the barn. The men joked as they worked; they didn't seem to mind getting wet at all. It was probably heavenly after working in the blazing hot sun in the hayfields and the suffocating heat of the haymows.

Mom was joyful, too, as her roses were already perking up. We saw several farm families heading for town. They all waved and tooted at us as they went by. Farmers always head for town when it rains; guess they don't feel guilty at a time like this. They live by the adage, "Make hay when the sun shines."

We played in the rain all afternoon and enjoyed every minute of it. It was wonderful not to have to pray for it anymore. At first the rain was warm, but later it seemed chilly. When we got goose pimples and our teeth began to chatter, Mom brought us some old bath towels to wrap around ourselves and dry our feet so that we could go in the house and get changed before we caught a cold or something.

The heat had made us all drag around, and our tempers seemed to flare more on hot humid days. But after our fun in the rain, we felt refreshed and clean. The grown-ups all seemed happy again, too.

The rain fell softly all night—we could hear the raindrops pitter-patter on the tin roof of the woodshed on the back of the house. Mom and Dad said the rain was a godsend; it would perk up the crops, the vegetables and flowers. The empty streams would run again and Gramps wouldn't talk about crop failures and wells going dry. The whole countryside was sparkling clean and freshly scented.

As I look back on my childhood days, I see that children got so much enjoyment from the simple things in life. We did not have swimming pools, but we enjoyed playing in the rain. Even swimming in the tiny creek in the woods was pure enchantment.

When my husband was perhaps 5 or 6, he and his little brothers took off all their clothing while playing in the cow barn so that they could play out in a rainstorm without getting their clothing wet. They had so much fun running back and forth between the barn and the sheds. But then their mother spotted them running nude in the rain while some neighbor ladies rode by in their horse-drawn buggy. Mother was slightly embarrassed and gave them a good talking-to—but later they overheard her telling that she couldn't help laughing at their antics, and that the neighbor ladies found their frolicking in the rain amusing, too. ❖

John Slobodnik

The Cold Thanksgiving

By Wyatt Cullom

Thanksgiving Day was always special for us when I lived in the country. I never remembered having turkey on that special day, but Mama always cooked a big, fat hen. We also had good old smokehouse ham that Dad had prepared "the old-fashioned way."

The morning was cold and the sky was overcast with gray clouds. Papa was busy getting Old Bill, our only means of transportation, hitched to the wagon.

"Where are you goin', Pa?" I asked, eager to go along with him.

"Over to Darlington," he answered. "I promised a friend of mine that I would bring him a ham for Thanksgiving."

"Can I go, Pa?" I asked.

"Looks like bad weather is brewing," he replied. "Maybe it will be too cold for you."

"Oh no, I can wear my stocking cap," I answered excitedly. "I won't get cold."

The 7-mile trip to Darlington wasn't too bad, but as we headed homeward, light rain began to fall. The crisp north wind was cold on my face. Very soon, the rain changed into small pellets of ice that bounced like tiny marbles on the wagon floor.

"Are you cold, Son?" Dad asked.

I didn't have to answer; just an upward glance at him was sufficient. I had already pulled my stocking cap down over my ears and I was crouching close to Dad for comfort. The rain was freezing on all the trees and shrubs. The biting north wind sent chills up and down my back. Ice was forming on the wagon floor, too, as Old Bill tramped slowly and cautiously along the frozen path.

My new sweater and stocking cap were not sufficient protection against the icy wind and freezing rain. So, just as a hen would spread her wings over her brood to protect them, Dad unbuttoned his warm overcoat and wrapped it around my cold shoulders. This act of love and concern gave me much relief.

As we traveled slowly, with the wind moaning through the ice-covered trees, Dad said, "Just hold on a little longer, Son. We will soon be home."

His encouragement gave me new comfort. I realized that there would be a warm fire awaiting us. But the greatest joy was that today was Thanksgiving Day! I knew that Mother had the table already spread with good things to eat.

As Old Bill labored to get us over the last hill, vapor streaming into the cold air from his nostrils, we could see the smoke boiling up out of the chimney. It was a welcome sight for a cold and weary child. ❖

So Cold, So Wet, So Windy

By Joseph W. Murray

When they elected the new president, all the talk at the general store turned to his promised New Deal. It was accepted that with things as they stood, any action would be an improvement. Most folks were content to have a new crop of politicians to complain about—business as usual.

Our part of the world had escaped the worst of the Dust Bowl years, but the weather managed to throw us a curve or two before the situation improved. It was the season just after that "New Deal" got elected that we remember as "The Winter It Got so Cold."

Down on the farm, we muddled though the chill as best we could. The mud had frozen solid by the first week of November, so you'd have to say we skated along over the top of it, convinced that things would surely be better by next August.

Fast following "The Winter It Got so Cold" came "The Wettest Spring in Memory." By the time it got warm enough to plant anything, Pa figured it was too late.

Truth to tell, no one at our place ever knew how cold it got that year. We kept a thermometer outside the kitchen window as a sort of early warning device for chilly mornings. Well, "The Winter It Got so Cold," the red liquid in that glass tube kept shrinking smaller and smaller until one morning, we looked out to find it had completely vanished. We all wore extra socks and mittens after that, just to be on the safe side.

One thing for sure: That "Winter It Got so Cold," we had to chip the pigs.

If you know pigs at all, you know they love to wallow in mud. They do this in summer to keep cool and in winter they do it mainly from force of habit. During "The Winter It Got so Cold," they'd get their living quarters all muddied up to pig perfection, then fall asleep in the ooze. Next morning, we'd find the entire herd frozen up just as fast as you please, squealing something terrible until somebody went in with a chisel and chipped them free. That's how you chip pigs.

A few of us worried that all those New Deal jobs would mean higher income taxes. We all felt a little better when someone realized that in order to pay higher taxes, we'd have to be earning more income. We reckoned that farming might never get us rich, but it would always get us by. Locally, there were other things that required attention.

Fast following "The Winter It Got so Cold" came "The Wettest Spring in Memory." By the time it got warm enough to plant anything, Pa figured it was too late to put in fish, but that's about how wet it was. The farmer down the road from our place decided to try fish farming that year (but then, he used to be a city boy, and he had a lot of strange notions). As it was, he lost the entire crop. He figured it was because he planted the fish too close together.

On our farm, we had to use a boat to get the potatoes planted—the field was that wet. The job went slower than planned because as we were planting each piece, we had to tie a rock to it for an anchor.

We escaped the worst of the flooding that year. There were only one or two days when the water table was higher than the kitchen table.

Summer that year turned into a fairly pleasant fall, if you forget about the wind. It came blowing straight out of the south. In these parts, that means more rain!

The wind wasn't really that strong; if you were driving the tractor, you could move against it most of the time. One particular fall morning, we were headed through the pasture down toward the potato field (which was still quite muddy). Through the wet and drizzle, there appeared a flock of five Canadian geese, their beaks pointed due south, no doubt bent on spending Thanksgiving in Miami. With the wind blowing against them and the visibility about as poor as it could get, those birds were flying perilously low. As the tractor drew alongside them, they were cruising no higher than the barbed-wire fence we had to build that spring to keep the cattle from swimming in the potato field.

Farmers are a sharp-eyed lot when it comes to spotting anything out of the ordinary. In the rain and wind, those birds were flying almost blind and no doubt deaf as well. It was possible to drive the tractor over so close that we could have reached out and touched one. I couldn't fail to notice that some environmental fellow had put a little tag on the legs of two of those geese. Just for fun, I wrote one of the numbers on a scrap of paper.

That morning was spent getting the tractor stuck in the middle of the potato field, then getting it unstuck only to mire down somewhere else. After a couple of hours, it seemed pointless to continue. So we began the drive out of the muck and back toward the pasture.

Did I mention that Canadian geese are strong birds? Did you know that they have a stubborn streak?

As the tractor came to the fence, there were those same five birds, still flapping their best, trying to get over the fence. A brief hunt through my wet coverall pockets revealed my scrap of paper. Sure enough! The number on the lead bird's tag matched the one I'd put down earlier that morning. It was that windy! ❖

Surviving the Blue Norther

By J.B. Cearley

They called it a "blue norther," but I thought of it as a terrible blizzard. It came screaming down across the Great Plains of Northwest Texas in early January 1932. The wind hit us first, roaring along at 40 miles an hour in the late afternoon. The old-timers laughed and said it was just a blue norther, a frequent occurrence on the plains.

They didn't laugh the next day. The wind had continued to blow all night, racing across the plains from the snowcapped Rocky Mountains. When we got up the next morning it was bitterly cold and cloudy. We three boys hurried through the morning milking, then we went off to school, 3½ miles away.

Getting water was much easier than climbing that old ladder and dipping water from the tank. We simply filled the buckets.

That little norther didn't let up like some folks predicted. The wind continued at 40 miles per hour, and about noon, some clouds began spitting snow. It was a peculiar kind of snow, light and dry as hen feathers in July. The teachers at New Lynn school would not let us outside for recess and noon break. The principal looked at the old thermometer and said it had been dropping all day. When school let out at 4 o'clock, it was down to 10 degrees. He dismissed school until the "little cold snap" was over.

As we jogged home, my two brothers and I felt like we were tromping about on the North Pole. Never had we been so cold. Our clothing was not adequate for such a cold, windy, snowy afternoon. Our hands and ears were nearly frostbitten when we arrived home.

We donned our work clothes and did the milking. Dad gave all the stock extra hay because of the cold. He took the old ax and chopped the block of ice on the stock water trough. They all shoved toward the icy water, trying to get a drink.

Our old house was so cold that Dad had us bring in some pine lumber scraps we had cut up to start the fires in the small stove we used to heat the living room. The fire had died down while we were outside. We had some mesquite shrubs and a sack of coal for fuel.

We used too much of the pine to start the fire. The blaze began roaring and got so hot that the stove turned red from the heat. Dad cut the damper on the stovepipe, afraid the house might catch fire. We finally got the stove regulated so that it was throwing off good heat. After supper, we sat humped up around the stove, listening to the old Belmot radio. We draped quilts over our legs because the wind was whistling through every crack in the old rented house.

We went to bed early because of the cold. The heat soon died out in the stove, and the blizzard crept into the house as the temperature continued to drop. Sometime during the night, Mother got up and spread all the extra bedcovers she could find over us. We felt warmer.

Early the next morning, Dad got up and started the fire in the stove. He lit all the burners in the kerosene stove in the kitchen. After 30 minutes, we all had to get up. The livestock needed attention.

I glanced outside to see that the wind was still blowing hard, driving the fluffy snow across the flat terrain. Dad turned the radio on and we soon learned that it was 15 degrees below zero. Never had I been in such cold!

Mother made hot biscuits for breakfast. The scrambled eggs and those hot buttered biscuits with homemade jam made us feel a little warmer.

Then it was time to do the milking. We

hurried through feeding and milking the six cows and carried the milk to the house and ran it through the cream separator.

Then we got some bad news. "Boys," Dad said softly, "we have a chore to do. The stock must have water, and there isn't any running from the storage tank to the stock trough. Everything is frozen."

We put on our heavy clothes and went outside into the blizzard. I looked around, shivering in the biting wind, and saw that most of the snow was being blown against the tumbleweeds along the fencerows. We wouldn't get enough moisture from the snow to wet a hat.

We clumped over to the windmill. Dad asked, "Where's the old ladder?"

Alvin, my older brother, said, "It's out by the stack of bundle feed. We had it there capping off that mountain of feed."

"You boys get it," Dad said, studying the tall overhead tank.

"How'll we get water for the stock?" I asked Brother as we went for the ladder.

"I don't know. The water pipes on the windmill are all frozen."

We brought the ladder and Dad directed us to set it against the storage tank. Then he turned to me. "Since you're the lightest, you'll have to climb the ladder and let the water down to us. We'll carry the buckets to the stock."

He had two large, 3-gallon buckets. He tied a rope to each bucket and handed me the ax. "You'll have to chop a hole in the ice big enough to get the water. Then you can fill the buckets with water."

I took the ax and the end of one of the ropes and started up the rickety ladder. Before I reached the top, one of the rotten rungs broke under my weight, and I fell to the ground while desperately trying to catch hold of the ladder.

"You all right?" Dad asked as I struggled to my feet.

"No. I broke my pride," I told him.

When Brother saw I didn't have any broken bones, he began laughing. "Why did you step on that rotten board? You should have known it would break," he laughed.

"Because I like to fall off ladders in a blizzard!" I told him, a little angry.

Dad spoke impatiently. "Shinny back up the ladder before we all freeze. The stock are thirsty."

I climbed the ladder, cautiously this time, and finally reached the top of the storage tank. Fortunately, the tank was nearly full of water. When I hit the frozen surface with the ax, it bounced up like I had struck concrete. I grabbed the ax handle with both hands and slammed the blade against the ice. A few small flakes of ice broke free. I chopped at the ice some 15 times as hard as I could, and then finally punched a small hole in the 5-inch-thick ice. After beating the ice with the ax for another 10 minutes, I had a hole large enough for the bucket.

The filled bucket, I discovered, was quite heavy. I heaved it up and over the top of the tank, spilling icy water on my clothes. I took the rope and let it slide down to Dad. He turned to take it to the stock, but they smelled the water and came running for it.

We worked for more than 30 minutes before the four horses, six cows and four calves were satisfied. Then Dad called to me, "Get a bucket of water for the chickens." They were thirsty, too.

By this time, ice was hanging from my clothes and my fingers and toes were really cold. I eased down the ladder and ran to the house where I shed my clothes and began warming my nearly frozen hands and feet. I had never imagined how much water a thirsty cow or mule could drink. We must have given them 20 buckets of water before the stock's thirst was quenched.

I glanced outside to see that the wind was driving the fluffy snow across the flat terrain. It was 15 degrees below zero, never had I been in such cold!

The cold would not have been so bad except for the wind. The only good thing the wind did was turn the old wind charger so we could use the one light in the family room and have power for the radio. If it was totally calm for three days—a rarity for West Texas—the battery would run down. Then we did not have electricity for the light and radio.

It was still bitterly cold the next morning, but the wind had dropped off to 20 miles per hour. Again, we had to get water from the storage tank for the stock.

Late that afternoon, the sun came out and the wind died down to tiny puffs. Dad told me and my older brother, "We'd better get out there and try to thaw out the windmill. The stock must have plenty of water."

That proved to be a challenging job. We removed the boards and the packing from the hydrant. Dad got a burlap bag and soaked it in kerosene. After he wrapped it around the pipe, he struck a match to it. I thought it would thaw the ice in the pipe in a minute, but when we turned the windmill wheel so it could catch the gentle breeze, the mill could

not lift the frozen ice in the pipe. Dad cut the mill off quickly.

He shook his head. "We'll have to use more heat," he said. "That ice is solid around the sucker rods in the pipe."

We got some more sacks and the newspapers from the house. Dad found some scrap lumber and we built a fire on the ground around the bottom of the pipe. After 20 minutes, the ice finally melted and the mill began to pump water.

Now getting water was much easier than climbing that old ladder and dipping water from the tank. We simply filled the buckets at the hydrant, then set them on the ground so the stock could drink their fill.

The next day we used the last of the coal. It was still too cold to dare to drive the Model-A 16 miles to town for supplies. Antifreeze had not made its way to West Texas, and we knew the radiator would be sure to freeze. "What'll we do for heat?" I asked Dad.

"You boys go to that pile of old fence posts and cut up about 10 of them. That will last through the day. Then we'll try and get to town tomorrow."

Another day arrived and it was not so cold. The norther was drifting out of the area. After working for three hours, we got the water line thawed so the stock tank filled with water from the underground pipes.

I felt a little sad as I watched the stock trying to drink from the slowly filling tank. I knew they had not had enough water for three days. The water we gave them helped them survive, but it was not adequate. The old cows were off in their milk and it would take three weeks for them to return to normal.

It was two more days before we could return to school; we missed a week all together. The school's water supply was also frozen, and the heating plant could not combat the zero weather.

After 10 days of terrible weather, things returned to normal and we got back to school. Fortunately, none of us became sick as a result of that West Texas "blue norther." ❖

Snowbound

By Frank M. Eastman

*I*t was cold that February day in 1919. The only sound was the chucking of wagon wheels on their axles and the steel rims squeaking on the frozen snow. Father had sold some of our belongings at an auction sale and all that remained was loaded on our wagons.

We hadn't heard of genes back in those days, but I suppose the pioneer spirit may have been passed down to Father, for he usually moved his family every two or three years.

It was too cold to sit on the seat high on the wagon, so my older brothers and I tied the ends of the traces together and draped them over the shoulders of our sheep-lined coats while we walked beside the wagons. I remember how my upturned collar was rimmed with frost and my eyes watered from the bitter cold. It wasn't easy, but I stomped my feet and flexed my fingers inside my bulky mittens to keep them from freezing.

The miles were long, but we had to get to the railroad station where the livestock could be cared for, and where we could find warmth and comfort. I was only 13, but I felt real grown-up driving the team by myself. I was getting colder and colder, so when my oldest brother, Monroe, caught up to us with his Model-T Ford, I was glad to be a boy again and let Mother tuck me in with a warm blanket. Father said my team was gentle and he would lead them behind another wagon.

I thought Monroe was some kind of a hero, for he had been in the war over in France. I didn't know what to say to him. Mother said he was just the same as he had always been. He told us he had never seen the enemy, although he had been ordered to fire his machine gun twice. I didn't know what a machine gun looked like, but I sure was glad to ride in his car.

Mother was to stay with us children at Wayne's house (he was my second-oldest brother) for two or three days. Then Monroe would drive us to our new home. He did not want to stay longer because he felt he would be needed to help unload our freight cars and get everything in order again.

It took two long days for the men to load all our things in the two boxcars. It was like a big puzzle to find the best places for the horses and milk cows, and then the crates of Plymouth Rock hens, the cream separator and all the household goods. The wagon wheels were removed to make more room, then farm machinery and all kinds of things were packed in and around them. Father made sure it was packed securely; otherwise, when the locomotive bumped the cars to connect them together, everything might go sprawling. And with the expense of moving, we couldn't afford to have anything broken.

Monroe drove his Model-T the six miles from Wayne's house to Woonsocket so he could help with the loading. The second day, the snow started falling again and it drifted across the roads and fields. Monroe had to drive carefully to keep the Ford on the road.

It was dark when the car lights showed dimly on the falling snow as he drove into the familiar yard. Wayne opened the big doors to the driveway in the double corncrib. They brushed the snow off the car and parked it there, out of the storm. Monroe was worried. He knew the freight train had picked up our two "emigrant cars" and was on its way north to the town of Woolsey, 30 miles away.

The next morning was bright and almost clear. The sun tried hard to shine through the haze. Snowdrifts made interesting patterns everywhere. Mother had us look at the winter trees, their bare limbs beautifully decorated with a marshmallow frosting of inch-deep snow.

But Monroe did not think the snow was pretty, especially when it began snowing again and we could no longer see the trees. He told Mother it would be days before he could drive on the roads, so he had decided to walk the six miles to Woonsocket, then take the passenger train in hopes he would arrive in time to help with the unloading. When he told Mother I should go with him, it made me feel important and almost grown-up again.

Mother wrapped a sandwich and placed it in the pocket of my coat. Then we began to walk along the railroad track that passed Wayne's house. We followed the tracks all the way to Woonsocket. I had never walked a railroad track and it was not easy. Snow drifted over the rails in some places, and in others it had blown clear. They had not spaced the ties to accommodate my short steps. I tried to walk the rail as the snowflakes landed softly on my cheeks and eyes, but I lost my balance. The snow swirled in what appeared to be a long tunnel before us, and we seemed to be the only people in the big, white world.

We arrived at the depot long before the passenger train was due to arrive, only to learn that it was having trouble with the ice and snow. The depot agent could only say he expected it would arrive "soon."

The depot was much larger than our haymow. It seemed cavernous and cold. The big, cast-iron stove was red from a coal fire. We could warm ourselves one side at a time by standing near it and turning like a pig on a rotisserie. The clack of the telegraph was almost constant. The agent tapped out a message and made notes on his pad. It was all very mysterious.

I was very tired, but too excited to sleep. A switch engine was moving cars to make a new freight train. When it came by the depot, I saw that it was covered with frost and snow. The men came in to warm their hands, and when they returned to the engine, its cold wheels spun on the frosty tracks.

I do not know when I fell asleep on a hard bench near the stove, but when Monroe woke me and said our train was coming, it was 5 a.m. During the night, Monroe had learned that the cars with our livestock and possessions were snowbound at Woolsey. We were moving all the way to a farm near Pierre, S.D., and our cars had to be switched to another railroad going west.

Because the steam line was frozen, the passenger train was as cold as the depot. But we did not mind it for the 30 miles we would ride.

Woolsey was a small prairie town, and still is for that matter, even though it is well over 100 years old. There were 13 cars, including ours, sitting on the siding, waiting for snow to be cleared from the tracks. The one small hotel was filled, and women and children huddled with warm blankets on the hard benches and slept curled up on the cold floor. Some of the men slept in the railroad cars to quiet the restless cows and horses. It was probably a bit warmer in with the animals anyway.

It was an endless, difficult task to feed and water the livestock and milk the cows twice a day. I suppose it was because everyone was so tired that it seemed funny, and people laughed when freshly laid eggs were found in the hen crates.

For three days, the emigrant cars sat and waited for snowplows to clear the tracks. Then, late in the afternoon, they hooked up the cars and we were on our way to our new home. ❖

The Evening Forecast, Brought to You by Nature

Predicting the weather is easy if you know how to read the signs.

By Mildred Klein

A long time ago, predicting the weather depended on a sense of awareness of the world around us. My parents, like their parents and grandparents, foretold the weather by looking at the sky, reading their own feelings and senses, and observing animal behavior.

When the farm animals became restless and bellowed and clamored, everyone was prepared to batten down the hatches. The pig was the best weather sage of all. It was said that pigs are the only creatures that "see the wind." According to myth, "When pigs squeal in winter, there will be a blizzard. When pigs carry sticks it will rain, and when they lie in the mud, there will be a dry spell."

When the cat sat by the fire more than usual or licked its feet, some people expected rain. When dogs began to dig holes, howled when someone went out, ate grass or refused meat, that too was a sign that rain was on the way.

Did you know that geese honk before it storms, that woodpeckers peck more furiously, that "rain crows" call for rain, and that robins stay close to their nests?

Insects were the most consistent of God's creatures. You might call the cricket the "poor man's thermometer." If you count the chirps he makes in 25 seconds, then add 37 to that number, you will get the correct temperature in degrees Fahrenheit.

Ants, too, foretell the weather. Expect stormy weather if they travel in lines and fair weather if they scatter. And watch the spiders. If they spin their webs in the morning you can expect a fair day. If they destroy the webs, a storm will soon follow.

An ancient weather saying is, "A storm makes its first announcement down the chimney." I learned at an early age that noise is a good weather indicator. Faraway sounds such as train whistles and distant birdcalls sound more mellow, as if coming though a long tunnel, before an extended spell of rain. Our sense of smell is keener also before rain.

Just as we do today, folks complained that their bodies were barometers that indicated changes in weather. A coming storm affected bones, joints, muscles, sinuses—even teeth and bunions. Blood pressure and changes in pulse also occurred.

I remember my father closely watching the big, black, rooster weather vane atop our tall windmill. He knew that when the wind began to shift, there would be a change in the weather. A wind changing to a clockwise motion—a veering wind—meant better weather ahead. If the wind shifted to a counterclockwise direction, a backing wind, bad weather was on the way.

The color of the sky, the clouds, the moon and stars all gave hints of the impending weather. Even today, when I see a pink glow in the sunrise or sunset I remember the little verse I learned as a child:

Red sky at morning,
Sailors take warning.
Red sky at night,
Sailors delight.

If I see a crescent moon tilted and showing a faint circle around it, I recall being told, "A moon with a circle brings water in its beak." A crescent moon lying on its back was a sign of dry weather.

Of course today we need only turn on our radio or television to get the weather forecast. But by developing our own weather wisdom, as our parents and ancestors did, we may find living in God's world a bit more provocative and gain a better understanding of those who lived before us. The weather sayings that have been handed down are a part of our heritage, just like the old weather vanes we see in museums and antique shops.

So look up to the sky and all around you. Feel the wind and tell the weather! ❖

Grandpa Jones Used to Say

By Nelle Portrey Davis

odern meteorologists might not put much stock in Grandpa Jones' forecasts, but for 80 years he lived by them. Most of his prophecies regarding the weather were presaged by, "As my pappy allus said," or, "As Granny Olds usta say … ." The sayings had been brought with the Jones family when they came west to the Ozarks through the Cumberland Gap, 175 years ago, and were handed down from one generation to the next.

There were many signs of a severe winter, and this wizened little mountaineer seemed to know them all: an unusual amount of fat on the tripe when beef was butchered; extra-heavy husks on the corn; squirrels hiding their winter store in hollow trees; and bees unusually busy, late in the summer. On the other hand, if nuts and acorns were found in a pile at the base of a tree, under or inside a fallen log, or some other hiding place close to the ground, it was a sign there would be little or no snow.

Grandpa Jones could always advise his listeners as to what the forthcoming day would bring: "Goin' to hev snow afore night. See them flocks of snowbirds pickin' up gravel?" Or, "Look at them lambs and calves playin' and cavortin' around. That's the sign of a storm."

A dewy morning indicated a sunny day:

When morning comes and grass is wet
Another day of sunshine yet,
But let the morning grass be dry,
A rainy day in the by and by.

A "sun dog" on each side of the setting sun on a winter evening foretold colder weather. Another of the old jingles predicting snow went:

Curdled sky in late December, in western sky,
Let man upon the earth remember snow will fly.

Threatening winds and gales were forecast in various ways. Perhaps this one was brought from England. It was current among the settlers of our own East Coast:

Mackerel skies and mares' tails
Make high ships carry low sails.

Watching the sky for portents brings to mind the oft-quoted prophecy, "When there is a circle around the moon, count the stars inside the circle. It will be that many days before a storm." And we remember how, in *The Wreck of the Hesperus*, the salty old sailor warned the captain of an impending storm:

Then up spake an old sailor,
Had sailed to the Spanish Main,

"I pray thee put into yonder port,
For I fear a hurricane,
Last night the moon had a golden ring,
And tonight no moon we see.

The direction of the wind might also foretell high winds or a good day.

Since so many of the jingles hint at sea conditions, it is safe to suppose that they originated with folk who depended on fishing for their livelihood:

When the wind is in the east,
'Tis neither good for man nor beast.
When the wind is in the north,
The skillful fisher goes not forth.
When the wind is in the west,
Then 'tis at the very best.
When the wind is in the south,
It blows the bait in fishes' mouth.

Summer showers quickly over were indicated when:

Clouds appear like rocks and towers,
The earth's refreshed by frequent showers.

Or,

Rain before 7, clear 'fore 11.

Another sign, Grandpa Jones used to say, of a rain shower's short duration was if a shower begins and the chickens stay out in it, it won't last long. And:

Sunshine and rain will soon come again,
But sunshine and shower won't last an hour.

Everyone should know that when the flickers (called "rain crows") call in the evening, they are calling for rain. When sounds carry afar—when the neighborhood children can be heard from a distance—it is a sign of rain.

Here's another oft-repeated Grandpa Jones jingle:

Grandma says (I guess it's true),
"There's sure a storm a-brewin'.
My jints are achin' through and through,
And houseflies are a-chewin'."

Another variation of the "red-sky" prophecy goes as follows:

Evening red and morning gray,
Send the sailor on his way;
Evening gray and morning red,
Bring down rains upon his head.
Evening gray and morning red,
The lamb and ewe go wet to bed.

And last of all is a truism we all recognize:

When the days at last begin to lengthen,
The cold of winter begins to strengthen. ❖

Healthful & Helpful Hints

Chapter Four

I am still amazed when I think of where the world is today compared to the world into which I was born. When Janice and I were born there were still a lot of folks—particularly out on the farm like our families—who still didn't have electricity.

The all-too-familiar trek to the outhouse was a part of my life until I was almost 12. Janice was a freshman in high school before the "luxury" of running water was added to her family's humble farm home.

Like other marvels of the modern world, medical science also amazes me. Today they can look inside a person and diagnose maladies we never would have even thought of back in the Good Old Days.

"An apple a day keeps the doctor away." That was how much we knew about such things back then. Wanting at all costs to avoid a visit from the doctor, there was hardly ever a day that we didn't pluck a fresh one off the apple trees halfway between our house and Grandma Stamps'. (And if there weren't any on our trees, we could always sneak up to Miz Jones' and get a couple on the sly.)

That saying must have worked because it was almost unheard of for us to call for the doctor. Maybe that's because we didn't have a telephone to call one. A trip into town was the only way of getting to the doctor, and we had to be sick nigh unto death to take that drastic step.

I grew up in an area and an era when the doctor was literally the last person you would see when you were sick. The first was Mama; if she couldn't handle the situation, Grandma was called in, followed by the granny woman up the road about a quarter-mile. Finally, if all else failed, Doc Evans was contacted.

Today—I have to admit it—I still tend to make the doctor's office the court of last resort. Janice and I have a small herb garden in which we grow everything from comfrey to garlic to peppermint. We cut sassafras roots in the late winter and drink tea from it the remainder of the season to ward off colds and other maladies. I take cayenne to help keep my blood pressure down, and Janice still fixes me a hot cup of chamomile tea if my stomach acts up. (I've never taken a drugstore antacid in my life.)

That apple a day taught me a few other things as well. I always was a little suspicious of all the preservatives being put into foodstuffs. One old-timer I used to spin yarns with had a simple motto for diet: "Eat only what will spoil—before it does." After he said it the first time, the more I thought about it, the more sense it made. In today's rush to create food with longer shelf life, perhaps if we heeded his words we would live healthier lives.

Now my folks could store our crop of apples in the root cellar for quite a while after harvest, but sooner or later we would have some spoil. With that in mind Mama taught me a valuable social lesson.

"One rotten apple in the barrel spoils the lot," she told me one day when I had started hanging around a roughneck from school. I knew she wasn't talking about fruit. She was warning me that I could get into a barrel of trouble hanging around that rotten apple. The message stuck.

So apples taught me about health and helped me make some good decisions. They also allowed countless boys to show off their manhood the first time they split one in half with their bare hands.

And they let girls know who was in their destiny by counting the number of twists on the stem before it gave way. "A … B … C …" How Janice's stem made it through 11 twists to that K for Ken, I'll never know.

Yes, an apple a day kept the doctor away. And, like the stories in this chapter, the apple also provided me healthful and helpful hints for life in the Good Old Days.

—Ken Tate

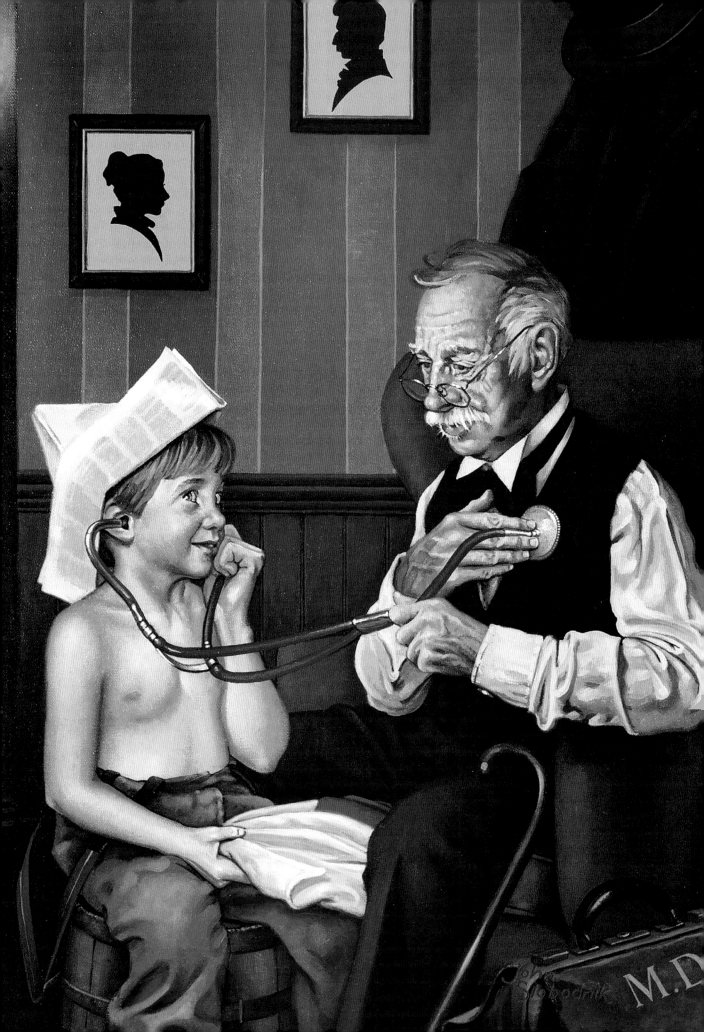

Just What the Doctor Ordered

Author Unknown

Addie Smith peered into the mouth of her two-month-old baby girl. She could see a dirty white crust around the baby's swollen gums. The tiny child was getting thinner every day since the thrush had first appeared, making it painful for her to eat. Anxiously, Addie hugged the baby tightly, wishing the rash was in her own mouth instead of her baby's.

What if this baby dies, too? Addie asked herself. Abruptly she checked the awful thought. Dr. Schnieder had warned her against thinking like that. Such thoughts were harmful to the mother's peace of mind and dangerous to the baby's health. He had told her how the mother's very thoughts were transferred into her milk and then into the baby's mind. Addie had tried to be very careful to think only healthy thoughts, but some fears had crept into her mind and apparently into the milk. And here was the result for all the world to see in her baby's mouth. If she took her baby in to see Dr. Schnieder, he would give her an awful scolding.

Only days before, Addie had taken the baby to the "granny lady" who had delivered many of the babies in the area. The old woman had looked in the mouth and promised to bring over a cure. Later, the granny lady had shown up with Willie Davis, a small boy who had never seen his father. The granny lady had Willie blow into the baby's mouth. It was a time-honored cure, but apparently it was not working like it was supposed to.

As the 20th century dawned, medical science called for physicians to treat the patient with more balanced care. Enlightened medical minds were now saying that "life-knowledge" was essential for good health.

When Addie's husband, Joe, came back from town, he brought news of a young doctor in a nearby village. They wrapped up the baby and took her immediately.

After the long buggy ride, it was suppertime and nearly dark when they arrived. The doctor and his wife were eating, but invited Joe and Addie to stay. Gratefully, the young couple accepted.

Throughout the meal and during the course of getting acquainted, Addie fearfully told the young doctor and his wife about the thrush that was spreading in the baby's mouth. To their surprise, he didn't scold Addie for her bad thoughts. Instead, he calmly mixed some powders and placed them in a small white envelope.

"Mix a pinch of the powder in water and rinse out the baby's mouth with it several times a day," he instructed. "A week or two should take care of everything."

Addie curiously looked at the envelope. She wanted to ask, "What's in it?" but that was a question one never posed to doctors. One just took what they prescribed and did not ask questions. After all, the doctor always knew what was best.

Joe paid the doctor with several heads of cabbage and two dozen fresh eggs.

In several days, the baby's mouth was noticeably better. In two weeks, it was completely healed. Addie never did know what the mysterious powder was, but she was impressed by the miracles of modern medicine.

Two Schools of Medical Thought in the 1800s

In the 1800s, most physicians fell into one of two categories in regards to the origins of illness.

One school of thought contended that illness was mostly due to bad attitudes on the part of the afflicted. This led to a sufferer being told that his pain was "all in his head."

The other contended that sickness was a normal part of the body's eventual death. The doctors in this camp believed that there was little that could be done to prevent it; they could only hope to alleviate its symptoms.

As the 20th century dawned, medical science called for physicians to treat the patient with more balanced care. Enlightened medical minds were now saying that "life-knowledge" was essential for good health. If the person only understood how his body worked and gave the body what it needed, both physically and mentally, disease would become obsolete.

A leading advocate in the crusade for "life-knowledge" was Swiss-born Mary Ries Melendy, M.D., Ph.D. After immigrating to the United States and attending medical school, Dr. Melendy set up a practice in Chicago. After practicing for 25 years, Dr. Melendy boasted of a remarkable record. She claimed she never lost a single case in which she had been the original physician called!

Most of the following treatments are those prescribed by Dr. Melendy in her publication *Vivilore*. The treatments described are given for information only and are not intended to be followed as medical advice.

Dr. Melendy's Advice

To remedy cold feet and hands: More starch is needed in the patient's diet. They need to eat wheat, barley, corn, tapioca and especially rice. The starches will produce more body heat if eaten with a sugar such as maple, beet or cane sugar. Honey is also recommended. A vegetable oil, such as nut or olive oil, also improves the body's own heating system when eaten with a starch. Cornmeal is especially a good winter food if it is eaten with milk and eggs.

Hard water is essential for young people: Young people need the lime that is found in hard water to build up and preserve teeth and bone substance. Without lime, teeth will soften, crumble and decay early. Those advanced in years require less lime. In middle years, the diet should be changed so as not to overload the skeletal system.

Ice water should be avoided: Ice causes the mucous membrane of the stomach to become temporarily pale and bloodless. It checks or altogether suspends the flow of gastric juice. Iced drinks at meals interfere with digestion and the beauty of the complexion.

Earache: Instill a few drops of oil of mullein or sweet oil in the affected ear. Then apply hot compresses. Always wear a hat out-of-doors.

Acute bronchitis: Make a hot cornmeal poultice containing two tablespoons red pepper and one tablespoon ground mustard. Apply to the chest and change the poultice every six hours.

Headache: Boil bark from a willow tree. Strain and drink warm. (***Editor's Note:*** *Aspirin is made from an artificially produced chemical that is the same substance found naturally in willow bark.*)

Bleeding gums: Use a dogwood twig to clean your teeth, or rinse your mouth daily with water and a bit of quinine.

Tooth decay: Mix the following ingredients and use to brush teeth:

7 ounces precipitated chalk
7 ounces powdered castile soap
2½ ounces powdered orrisroot
½ drachm oil of peppermint
¼ drachm oil of cinnamon
Glycerin sufficient to form a paste

Follow brushing by cleaning between teeth with silk embroidery floss.

Black eye: Use a poultice of slippery elm bark mixed with milk. Put it on warm.

Baldness: Sickness, worry, excessive study, free exercise of passions or anything that exhausts the energy produces baldness. Rubbing or brushing or massaging the scalp until it is red will restore vitality to the follicles. An onion cut in two and then rubbed over the scalp day and night also proves successful.

Chilblains: Soak the affected part in alum mixed with as hot of water as can be borne for 20 minutes. Or, instead of water, use liquid in which unpeeled potatoes have been boiled.

To determine the sex of offspring: Count on the sex of the older or stronger parent to be transmitted. ❖

First Flower of Spring

By Francis X. Sculley

There is a tiny, quarter-sized member of the composite family known as *Tussilagofarfara*, affectionately known as the coltsfoot. Praised by most of the greats of medical history, the plant has been used to treat coughs and colds since pioneer days; in fact, tussilago means "cough dispeller."

The dandelion-shaped flower heads seem to pop from the ground like mushrooms. In fact, everything the little plant does, it does in reverse. Following the appearance of the flowers, stems appear, pushing the blossoms out into the raw March air. Then, as if to hide its nakedness, it reaches down and pulls up its leaves, which will, within a fortnight, acquire the shape of a horse's hoof—hence the name coltsfoot.

This flowery strip-tease in reverse may occur from late February to mid-April, depending on the locale. In Virginia and the Carolinas, it will often pop out of the ground late in February, while in New England, it may not appear until April.

It usually emerges before all the other spring plants except the skunk cabbage, and it will grow anywhere: on rocky embankments, the edges of concrete roads, even in cinder piles. It is virtually indestructible.

Coltsfoot Cough Drops

In New England and Europe, where people make their own cough drops, this simple recipe is suggested:

Boil an ounce of coltsfoot leaves in a pint of water. Add two cups of sugar to the strained liquid. Boil to the thread stage.

Pour into a greased tin; score before the candy is completely hard. (It will be as hard as concrete when finished.) ❖

Advice From the Almanac

The following was excerpted from the 1898 American Farmers Almanac. Various almanacs became the reference books of choice for farmers across the country. Today noted for their poetic weather prognostications, in those days of old, they were indispensable clearinghouses of helpful and healthful hints.

• Cutting off large limbs is best done by first sawing a little on the under side, so that when the limb falls it will not split the wood nor peel the bark down the trunk.

• Turnips are a natural feed for sheep and may safely be pastured, permitting the animals to eat all they desire. In fact, root crops are always good for any of our farm animals.

• In setting out trees, work the soil well to a good depth. This will enable the roots to go down a long way into the soil and find an unfailing supply of moisture.

• The farmer who thinks he can give up stock-growing is sure to find his mistake. The pastures must be utilized and the fertility of the farm maintained.

• Plan during June for an abundance of forage crops to supply the cows during the dry summer and fall months.

• Do not hang the harness in the stable if you can avoid it.

• It is poor economy to build a big barn and let a large portion of the room go to waste. Utilize every inch of the room.

• One advantage with winter dairying is that it affords a source of income when the farm yields but little revenue.

• A part of the small apples should be kept to feed the poultry in winter. This will pay better than making cider of them.

• There are almost as many varieties as there are different flowers that produce honey, and the difference in flavor is very perceptible.

• Do not try to see how many cows you can winter, but how many you can keep up to full production.

• All bare ground in the vicinity of the poultry yard should be seeded to rye, crimson clover or dwarf essex rape for fall, winter and spring pasture.

The Climatic Effect of Forests

The climatic effect of forests is hard to overestimate, and it is not possible with our present knowledge to say how much the temperature and moisture are affected by forests. But the temperature of a grove is lower in summer and higher in winter than that of the open plain. A hedge or belt of evergreens or deciduous trees shows a lower temperature on the windward than on the leeward side. The degree of moisture, too, in a grove or forest is higher than in an open field or plain. So the fact that both temperature and moisture of the air and soil are affected by forest growth is as clear as any fact in nature.

• Gather garden seeds as they ripen. Those that come early are best; label at once, and when dry and clean, store in a dry place away from mice.

• Feed at regular hours and at no other time. The flock will soon learn when to expect their meals and will forage contentedly the rest of the time.

• Annual pruning largely avoids the necessity for removing large limbs.

• Grapes thrive best in well-cultivated and well-drained land.

• Encourage the chickens to run in the orchard; they will get away with a great many injurious insects.

• The future shape of the tree depends largely upon the pruning given in its early life.

• New land is best adapted to the growth of berries.

• Fruit trees or plants will not take care of themselves.

• Cut away all grain growing within 4 or 5 feet of every young fruit tree; leave the cut grain lie for a mulch.

• Spring pigs, if given plenty of clover in the

first five months, will be ready for the butcher in October. They should be made to weigh about 300 pounds.

•   Fall growth of wood should not be stimulated in trees.

•   Thorough culture saves moisture and invigorates the plant, rendering it less susceptible to the attacks of insects and fungi.

•   Do not let your stock drink water that you would not drink yourself.

Keeping Sweet Potatoes

This is one farmer's experience of keeping sweet potatoes: "I gather my potatoes in boxes made of two pieces of 12-inch boards sawed off long enough for ends and common laths nailed on each side and the bottom, so that when complete they will hold a bushel, level full. I do not give size because I calculate the number of cubic inches in a bushel, and make them to fit a wagon body, three sitting side by side in width, and enough to fill the body in length, and put them two or three deep, sitting on one another owing to size of body. Pick them up in these boxes, then set them in wagon and carry home. It saves handling, and also measures your potatoes without bruising them so much. I have enough clean, dry sawdust on hand ready, also boxes and barrels sufficient to hold my crop.

"I make my boxes to hold not over 20 bushels, as that is enough in one bulk. Put sawdust in bottom, then a layer of potatoes, then sawdust alternating until box is full, then cover over the top with 5 or 6 inches of sawdust.

"Packing in sawdust is not an experiment with me. I have been keeping them thus for several years, and never lose any potatoes. If for any cause one should rot, the sawdust cakes

around it, absorbs the moisture, and does not communicate it to others."

•   Entirely too little attention is given to the shape and fitting qualities of the horse collars, particularly as to the width thereof. The collars should fit the sides of the neck closely without pinching.

•   Every farmer who has not an extensive range for his hogs should sow rye to give them a green winter feed.

•   Air and sunshine are health-giving to fowls as well as to people.

•   Ripened cream should be thick and smooth when put into the churn, not lumpy, neither sloppy.

Poultry Notes

Always feed ducks and turkeys where you want them to roost. When table scraps are fed to poultry, always try to feed them fresh. When the growth is to be pushed, the chickens should be fed every two or three hours.

Spare That Tree

It is well to think twice before cutting down a fine tree. Some claim that such a tree in a field is only "a big weed," but this is a narrow view. Possibly the hay crop may be slightly diminished, and the hoed crops will not yield quite as much as they otherwise would on account of the tree. But man ought to have some regard for the higher instincts of his nature. If he gets so that he can only see beauty in plants that have a cash value in the market he dwarfs his nobler faculties.

The man who should plant potatoes instead of flowers in front of his house would be looked upon as deficient in taste, and strangers, at least, would gain the impression that he was not only an intensely worldly man, but that he was also lacking in mental cultivation. The man who removes a splendid tree because it takes a few feet of ground from his field crops is doing himself and all about him an injury.

A fine tree is a great object lesson in the natural world. It also has a decided value as a home for birds—those greatly neglected friends of the farmer—and in its effects upon the soil and air.

- Apply one part Paris green and six parts flour when the vines are dry, and the cucumber beetle will leave. Sprinkle very lightly.
- The cellar should be kept as clean and dry and well ventilated as any other part of the house.
- Cover the horse's head if you have occasion to lead him out of a burning building.
- Turn down a clover sod for a big crop of late cabbage.

How to Measure Corn in a Crib, Hay in a Mow, Etc.

This rule will apply to a crib of any kind. Two cubic feet of sound, dry corn in the ear will make a bushel shelled. To get the quantity of shelled corn in a crib of corn in the ear, measure the length, breadth and the height of the crib, inside of the rail; multiply the length by the breadth and the product by the height; then divide the product by two, and you have the number of bushels in the crib.

To find the number of bushels of apples, potatoes, etc., in a bin, multiply the length, breadth and thickness together, and this by 8, and point off one figure in the product for decimals.

To find the amount of hay in a mow, allow 512 cubic feet for a ton, and it will come out very near correct.

- Poultry must have loose ground to scratch over; it does them good in various ways.
- Good corn fodder, good clover and good straw will make milk. The latter must be supplemented with grain, and the first two ought to be.
- Onions should be turned over every few days, and any which show signs of growing should be picked out.

Weeds as Fertilizers

Recent experiments conducted at the University of Virginia on the value of weeds as fertilizers have proved eminently instructive. The common pokeberry *(phytolacca decandra)* was found to be of the highest value to the agriculturist, a dry ton being found to be equal to manure that would cost $21.93 if the chemical matters, such as nitrogen, phosphoric acid and potash, had been purchased as fertilizers. Of the 50 plants examined, the common panic grass was found to be the lowest in the scale, it being found to have an economic value of but $3.40 per ton.

- Stables should be kept clean and dry. The manure should never be left in at night to deprive the horse of pure, sweet air.
- Nothing should hinder commencing the hay harvest as soon as the heads are formed, and a little before the blossom appears.

Salting Cows

Salting the cows is one of the little things that is sometimes lost sight of under the pressure of other, and what is regarded as more important work, but a trial recently made at the Mississippi Experiment Station indicates inattention to this point may be a rather expensive oversight. Three cows were kept without salt for four weeks, and their milk record kept during the last two weeks of this period; then they were given the usual allowance of salt for two weeks, and on comparing the milk records, it was found that the cows gave 454 pounds of milk during the first period when salt was withheld, and 564 pounds during the second, when salt was furnished, a difference of 110 pounds of milk in two weeks in favor of salting.

- Short rotation of crops and clean tillage practically do away with the old weed problem. The clover, for instance, is so heavy the first year that it hardly gets a foothold, and then do not wait until it runs out and the pests in, but turn it right over and put in a crop.
- The profitable dairy cow should give milk 10 months in the year.
- Throw dishwater around fruit trees, currants,

gooseberries, etc. Coffee grounds are said to be valuable when put around shrubbery and flowering plants.

• Better throw damaged fodder into the manure pile than to force stock to eat it. Do not try to save at the expense of your stock.
• Poultry like buckwheat and it makes an excellent change in their diet.
• Butter of prime quality should never be touched with the hands.
• Every farmer should raise a few carrots. You can feed at least a third less oats and the horse will do better.

Cream Temperature

Strange as it may seem, some housewives have not yet learned the use of the thermometer in butter making, and still rely upon the old "finger test," which in reality is no test at all. Meanwhile, in the hot days, the "butter spoon" will be in demand on some farmers' tables. Get a thermometer and know "where you are at." If you have no ice, use plenty of cold water around (not in) the milk and cream. Churn in early morn at as near 58 degrees as you can get it.

• Many successful swine growers we know rake up the corncobs, burn them, and when in the form of bright, live coals, throw water on a portion of the pile, thus making charcoal for the hogs to eat. A little salt may be added.
• The busiest hens are the best layers.
• There is no question but that there are some animals that possess the quality of a more perfect assimilation of food for the production of milk than others.
• Erect your poultry houses long before your chicks are ready for them. Clean the houses at least once a week, and sprinkle lime or land plaster over the floor.

Get a Reputation

It pays to get a reputation for a specialty in stock raising established, either for a farm or a district, for then buyers come direct to that locality for their purchases. This holds good in a larger scale, as witness the fame of Kentucky; her renown for horses has spread as far as Japan, and the agent of the Mikado's government has been a profitable patron. ❖

Grandpa Fritch's Salve

By Mrs. P.R. Viers

I remember well a salve my Grandpa Fritch made for our family. I hope it will be a help for others.

Grandpa Fritch said the recipe for the salve had been in his family since the early 1800s. I do know it is good for what ails you!

This salve was a staple in our collection of cures, along with castor oil, Epsom salts, sassafras, senna, catnip, peppermint and chamomile teas, skunk and goose grease (*ugh!*), onion poultices and hop syrup for coughs.

Once in a great while, for a bad cold, we were given a hot whiskey sling. It was made by mixing some sugar and a dash of whiskey in a cup, and then filling the cup with hot water. After we took this dose, we were put to bed with a hot brick or a bag of hot salt or wheat to sweat out the illness. Oh—I forgot about the strip of salt pork that was put around our necks for a sore throat, or on a sore to draw it … and a flaxseed in your eye if you happened to get a cinder from a train.

Guess that I was a little too young for sulphur and molasses, but I do remember wearing the "fetty bag" (asafetida) to scare away germs. At any rate, we lived through it, but I sometimes wonder how!

Grandpa Fritch's Salve.

1½ pounds lard
1 pound beeswax
1 handful of each of the following:
Elder bark
Sassafras bark
Mullein flowers
Jimson leaves
Tansy leaves
Yarrow leaves
Button weed
Plantain leaves

Make a tea of herbs and strain. Add the lard and beeswax and boil to the consistency of salve.

Fly Catchers

By Raymond E. French

By 1905, most people accepted the fact that many diseases were carried by germs. As a result, an interest in sanitation was sweeping the country.

During 1906, Samuel J. Crumbine, M.D., dean of the Kansas University School of Medicine, was investigating the cause of a typhoid epidemic. In the process, he noted that flies in Army mess halls and kitchens carried specks of a white powder used in and around the nearby garbage cans. After being appointed secretary of the Kansas State Board of Health in 1907, he started a campaign to rid the state of houseflies. The campaign was popularized by the slogan "Swat That Fly." The news and advertising media gave it a great deal of space as a public service.

About the same time, Frank A. Rose, superintendent of the schools of Weir, Kan., devised a "fly swatter." It was just a small piece of screen wire tacked to the end of a light stick 10–12 inches long. The schoolchildren of Weir were urged to make them, use them and sell them. They were soon available in every 5-and-10-cent store, grocery and hardware store, even drugstores.

Merchants began offering small prizes to the boy or girl who brought them the most dead flies. This brought creative fathers into the act. They devised and made "fly traps" to elevate the killing to a wholesale basis.

This fly trap was simple. It was just a top and bottom, round or 15–18 inches square. A hole in the top board was covered by a lid so the captured dead flies could be removed. A hole in the bottom board was generally round, about 6 inches in diameter, and covered with a screen wire cone 6–7 inches high, with a half-inch outlet in its top. The outlet opened into the body of the trap. Side—or corner—pieces holding the top and bottom together extended 3–4 inches below the trap, forming legs on which it stood. Then screen wire was wrapped around the trap and tacked tightly at top, bottom and each corner—or vertical—support.

When the trap was placed near garbage cans, manure piles, kitchen doors, or wherever flies congregated, it was baited with something—partially decayed meat scraps, perhaps a spoonful of honey, whatever was handy. This took them into the cone, from which there was no escape, except into the body of the trap.

The campaign spread rapidly all over the country. By the summer of 1908, the alleys of every town and city were dotted with fly traps. They were to be found around most barns, chicken houses, pig sties, manure piles and by the two-holer outhouses. During the following decade, our fly population was almost as low as it is now. There was less contagious disease, and infant mortality substantially decreased. ❖

A Sure Cure for Asthma

By Dale Denney

The Oklahoma dust storms in the mid-1930s made my asthma worse. At 11, I was the youngest of four boys in a family of eight.

It really made a full house when Aunt Edith and Uncle Leo came to stay with us for a few days on their vacation. They were rich, or so we thought. Uncle Leo had a steady job with an oil company. They lived rent-free in a lease house, had all their utilities furnished and drove a brand-new 1936 Ford coupe.

Mom gave them a bedroom to themselves and made pallets on the floor for those of us who had to give up our beds. But we didn't mind. The commotion was exciting.

Aunt Edith stepped out of the kitchen back door one morning and caught me coughing and wheezing on the back porch. "Land sakes, Lula," she exclaimed to Mom. "What's wrong with Dale?"

"Asthma," Mom said. "I try to keep him quiet, but he's so rambunctious."

"I know how to cure it," Aunt Edith said, "if you'll let him go home with me for a few weeks."

The thought of going home with Aunt Edith and Uncle Leo was almost more than I could bear. They had shiny new linoleum on their floors, a refrigerator with a light in it, and a big radio standing in the corner of their living room, which they turned on every night to listen to their favorite programs.

However, Mom was reluctant. She didn't want to impose. "Besides," she said, "he's so

I was always anxious to take my medicine because I loved opening the refrigerator door. I'd keep peeking in the crack to see if the light stayed on all the time or if it went off when I closed the door.

young. He'll get homesick."

I begged to go, vowing not to get homesick. Aunt Edith kept insisting. Mom finally gave in.

The 30-mile trip to their house was the longest, grandest journey I'd ever made. I couldn't keep from staring out the rear window, fascinated by the billows of dust we left behind as we barreled along the dirt road at 30 miles an hour.

When we got out at their house, the popping and pounding of the oil-well engines all around us on the lease sounded like a war zone. How could you sleep in all this racket? But I got used to it and slept just fine—after the first night.

I loved walking barefoot on Aunt Edith's cool, clean floors. Their furniture all looked new, and Aunt Edith had starched doilies on every arm of every chair.

We weren't there two hours before Aunt Edith mixed up a light brown liquid and poured it into a pint fruit jar. She gave me a teaspoon full. It had a queer taste. While it was sweet, like honey, it tasted sour, too; sort of a cross between lemon and vinegar.

"I want you to take a spoonful of this twice a day," she told me. She was stern about it, and I knew she meant business.

I was always anxious to take my medicine because I loved opening the refrigerator door. I'd keep peeking in the crack to see if the light stayed on all the time or if it went off when I closed the door. And all the wire shelves inside had food on them. It made me hungry just looking in it.

The best part of taking the medicine was Aunt Edith praising me when I did. She even made me feel good the way she gave me a

The Denney family a few years before my asthma "cure." That's me, front row left. Dad was a driller and helped bring in an Oklahoma oil field. We would have a house full when Aunt Edith came to visit us. I imagine Mom, with her large family to cook and care for, was more than happy to let me go home with Aunt Edith so she could try her secret asthma "cure" on me.

special job of carrying in water. She didn't want to have to tell me when we needed water, she said. It was up to me to keep an eye on the water pail. When the water level was low, I had to take a 3-gallon bucket and go across a field to one of the wells that pumped fresh water and fill the bucket and carry it back to the house.

I made my own special path through the grass from the house to the well and pretended I was on an African safari. I had to be on special lookout for lions and tigers and elephants and cannibals and things like that.

Carrying water to their house was lots more fun than pumping water out of our water well back home. At home, I pumped water just outside the kitchen door and people were always around. If you can't imagine things

while you work, work is work.

I enjoyed the way Aunt Edith petted me. She'd let me help her bake and do other things in the kitchen. And she'd stop to give me a hug for no reason at all. We even got to kissing one another.

One night after supper, Uncle Leo announced that we were all going into town to see a show. There was a Charlie Chan movie playing. He loved the smooth way Charlie Chan solved mysteries.

I'd been to the movies before, but not to a theater so grand as the one they went to. It was even air-conditioned! After it was over and we were on our way to the parked car, Aunt Edith put her arm around me and asked, "Did you like it, Honey?"

Honey? She called me Honey! I leaned against her soft body and said, "Yes. It was a lot of fun."

But Mom was right. I did get homesick. Aunt Edith caught me hiding in the bedroom, sniffling, one morning. She didn't ask me what was wrong. She knew. She came to me and pulled my head against her stomach and patted me gently. I put my arms around her. She was so soft and warm. I wanted to hug her like that forever. Soon my homesick feeling went away and I was all right.

Then one day we were in the kitchen and I went to the refrigerator to take my medicine. There wasn't much left. "Look," I said, holding up the jar proudly. "It's almost empty. You'd better make some more."

"Why?" she asked, a glint in her smiling eyes.

"Because … " I said, then paused when I realized what she meant by asking "why." I wasn't coughing and wheezing anymore and, thinking back, I hadn't been for a week or more. Then I knew I was cured. She laughed at the sheepish look on my face.

I suppose it could have been from the medicine she brewed up—from what I have no idea. It's more likely, however, that Aunt Edith's cure for my asthma came from the undivided love and attention she gave me. ❖

Indian Joe

By Charles Bryant O'Dooley

He called the earth "Mother" and believed that if man would treat the land with respect, it would always provide for his needs.

Indian Joe was a full-blooded Cherokee who lived alone in a log cabin he built himself on 200 acres of land. He worked long, hard hours on the railroad to save enough money to buy the land, which was well forested with huge oak, hickory and beech trees. It also had a natural lake and a stream with a beautiful waterfall. The only open space on the land was a spot big enough for the cabin, a garden and a chicken coop.

Let me tell you how I met Joe and how we became lifelong friends. I was 7 years old and Mom had sent me to the country store for a can of lye to make soap. It was midsummer. The road was hot and dusty as I trod along in bare feet. I got a cold drink from a roadside spring and sat there awhile to rest.

Suddenly, I heard someone playing a fiddle. It was like a cool stream running over the rocks, peaceful and serene and soothing. Turning my head in the direction of the music, I noticed a path leading from the spring through the woods. I followed it to investigate.

It was cool under the canopy of trees forming the roof of the path. After a thousand feet, I came to a clearing in the forest, and the sight is embedded in my mind to this day. There stood a log cabin like something I had seen in history books, with real mud between the logs for chinking and a stone chimney. To the side of the cabin was a well-tended garden. There was a small chicken coop out back, an old-fashioned outhouse and a porch running across the front of the cabin, which is where I first laid eyes on the man.

He was sitting on the porch playing a fiddle and didn't see me until I had almost walked up to him.

"Didn't see me, did you?" I said.

"I knew where you were when you left the spring and made your way to my cabin," he retorted. "Who are you, boy? Where d'you come from?"

I introduced myself and told him my name was Charlie.

"They call me Indian Joe. Come, I'll show you my home."

Inside was something you don't see today and probably never will. Every piece of furniture was hand-carved from trees. The table was made from logs split in half and smoothed with an adz. The chairs were fashioned from young hickory saplings. The bed frame was maple with rope laced across the bottom for springs. The cupboard was made from sassafras wood, and a log split in half formed a bench that held the water bucket. The big stone fireplace was rigged with iron hooks that could swing out over the fire and hold a cooking pot.

Even the dishes, forks and spoons were carved of wood. It was like taking a trip back in time. I stood there with my mouth open in awe.

"I make everything I need, and raise garden for food and hunt for meat. I made my fiddle and drum." I hadn't even noticed the drum, made from a piece of hollow log with animal skins stretched over both ends.

From that day on I spent all the time I could at Joe's house, listening to him play the fiddle and tell stories. He taught me to play the old-time tunes and told me a lot of folklore, like how to predict the weather.

One day as we were sitting on the porch, a woolly worm crawled across the steps. Joe took it in his hand: "See how the worm has small dark coloring at the front, then a pale patch in the middle and a large dark spot at the end?"

I nodded.

"The small dark spot at the front means winter will come early. The pale spot in the middle means we will have fairly mild weather in the middle of winter, and the dark spot at the end of the worm means we will have bad weather at the end of winter." And you know something? I have checked this out over the years and it almost always holds true.

Joe said that if you see a ring around the moon, it means rain within 24 hours. And it does, too. You can check it out for yourself. If the sun sets red in the evening, Joe said, "Red at night, farmer's delight; pretty day tomorrow." If the sun rose red in the morning, he said, "Red in morn, farmers be warned— rain before nightfall." This also holds true 95 percent of the time.

If his chickens stayed out in the rain instead of going inside, Joe said it was going to rain all day, and sure enough, it did. If the wild ducks and geese flew south earlier than usual, Joe predicted an early winter—and he was right. He told me animals had instincts that told them things people knew nothing about.

I came to a clearing in the forest, and the sight is embedded in my mind to this day. There stood a log cabin like something I had seen in history books, with real mud between the logs for chinking and a stone chimney.

One day Joe took me fishing near the waterfall. We caught several nice-size trout and he showed me how to prepare the fish for our dinner without a frying pan. He split the fish open and removed the insides, but left the scales on. After washing the fish, he stuffed some wild onion tops inside. Then he got some clay from the creek bank and wrapped each fish in it.

He built a fire, and when it had burned down to red coals, he placed the clay-wrapped fish on the coals and raked more hot coals over them with a stick. He left them there for about 15 minutes, then raked them out. When he removed the clay, the scales and skin came off, leaving the cooked white meat of the fish, which he placed on a piece of maple bark.

Joe showed me how to whittle arrows from hard hickory and make the bow from ash. He made the arrowheads from flint the way his forefathers had, by chipping and forming the flint with a larger stone. He split the end of the arrow and pushed the flint head into it, then wrapped it with rawhide. For the feathered end, he used wing feathers from his chickens. Joe always won prizes at the county fair with his hand-carved toys, dishes and tools.

Joe only took what he could use from the animal world and he only cut trees he would use to make things he needed. He called the earth "Mother" and said that if man would treat the land with respect, it would always provide for his needs.

Joe was one of the early conservationists in the way he respected and cared for the land. And Joe didn't smoke, drink alcohol or use salt. He used wild herbs to season his food.

When I reached the age of 18, I was drafted into the Army, but I kept in touch with Joe through letters, which he had my mother read to him. Then he told her what to write back to me.

Just before I was to be discharged, my mother wrote that Joe had passed away. In his will he left me his fiddle, drum, the big bow and arrows and several other things I had admired. His cabin and land were willed to the county with the stipulation that it be used for a park and that no trees were to be cut or the land disturbed. The county respected Joe's wishes. Today there are natural footpaths through the woods and only canoes are allowed on the lake. Joe's cabin was turned into a museum of sorts, with all his handcrafted objects displayed. I was appointed caretaker and, until I got married and moved away, I used to sit on the porch in the evening after the visitors had left and play the fiddle Joe left me.

One night in late fall, I was sitting on the porch with my thoughts buried in the past when I heard the honking of wild geese flying south for winter. They flew in a V shape, silhouetted against the full moon. I felt such peace and serenity, and I said without thinking, "There they go, Joe." And it seemed I felt his presence there beside me. ❖

Beauty Secrets

By Helen Colwell Oakley

If Mom would only buy the right soap, I knew I would be beautiful.

Editor's Note: While we learned so much from parents and grandparents back in the Good Old Days, often times we found ourselves drawn to the ways of the big city. Many times the newspapers and movie pulp magazines of the day brought us the titillating allure of Tinsel Town. Helen Colwell Oakley remembers when her country horse sense was augmented by the wisdom of the ways of the world at large. It was there she learned these beauty secrets.—K.T.

When I was growing up on the farm in New York in the late 1920s and 1930s, Mom swore by two well-known brands of soap: Ivory, for personal cleanliness and delicate cleaning jobs, and Octagon soap for laundry and tough cleaning jobs. Octagon soap was gold-colored. Ivory was pure white; it was considered to be nearly 100 percent pure, and it was the only soap on the market that could float.

For years, Mom bought nothing but these two fine soaps for our household. Granted, they did an excellent job of keeping our house spic and span, as well as helping all of us to be neat and clean, especially after a thorough scrubbing on Saturday night with a fresh cake of Mom's faithful Ivory.

But my girlfriends and I at the little one-room schoolhouse down the road read in the comic pages about the beautiful movie stars using Lux toilet soap. They looked so glamorous and alluring in the photos that my little friends and I wanted to be just like them.

I begged Mom to buy Lux toilet soap on our next trip to the grocery store in town, but she didn't like newfangled ideas, so it wasn't easy to win her over.

We all agreed: If Lux soap would do it, we girls wanted to begin using it right away.

I begged Mom to buy Lux toilet soap on our next trip to the grocery store in town, but she didn't like newfangled ideas, so it wasn't easy to win her over. "Look how pretty it's packaged," I said. "Smell the delightful, perfumed fragrance," I pleaded.

"Ten cents is quite a price to pay for a cake of soap," Mom said, mentioning that Ivory was much cheaper at 5 cents per cake, and much larger at that! But Mom finally agreed to let me try a cake of Lux soap, and I was in seventh heaven.

I savored each and every cake of Lux as I inhaled the delicate, perfumed scent at bath time. I basked in the sheer loveliness of the Lux beauty regimen practiced daily by the beautiful movie stars, as the papers stated.

Later on, I was informed that one could not always believe what one reads in the papers. Nevertheless, I'm sure the ads about the beautiful Lux movie stars inspired many budding beauties. I know they made my little friends and me aware of the necessity of a beauty-cleansing regimen if we wanted to grow up to be lovely and attractive.

The outcome of the story proves that little girls and teens alike need inspiring role models to encourage them to take good care of themselves in the formative years. My little friends and I grew up to be quite beautiful and were whisked away by our Prince Charmings. I like to think that the Lux ads played a magical part in our life stories. ❖

Modern Screen, May 1940

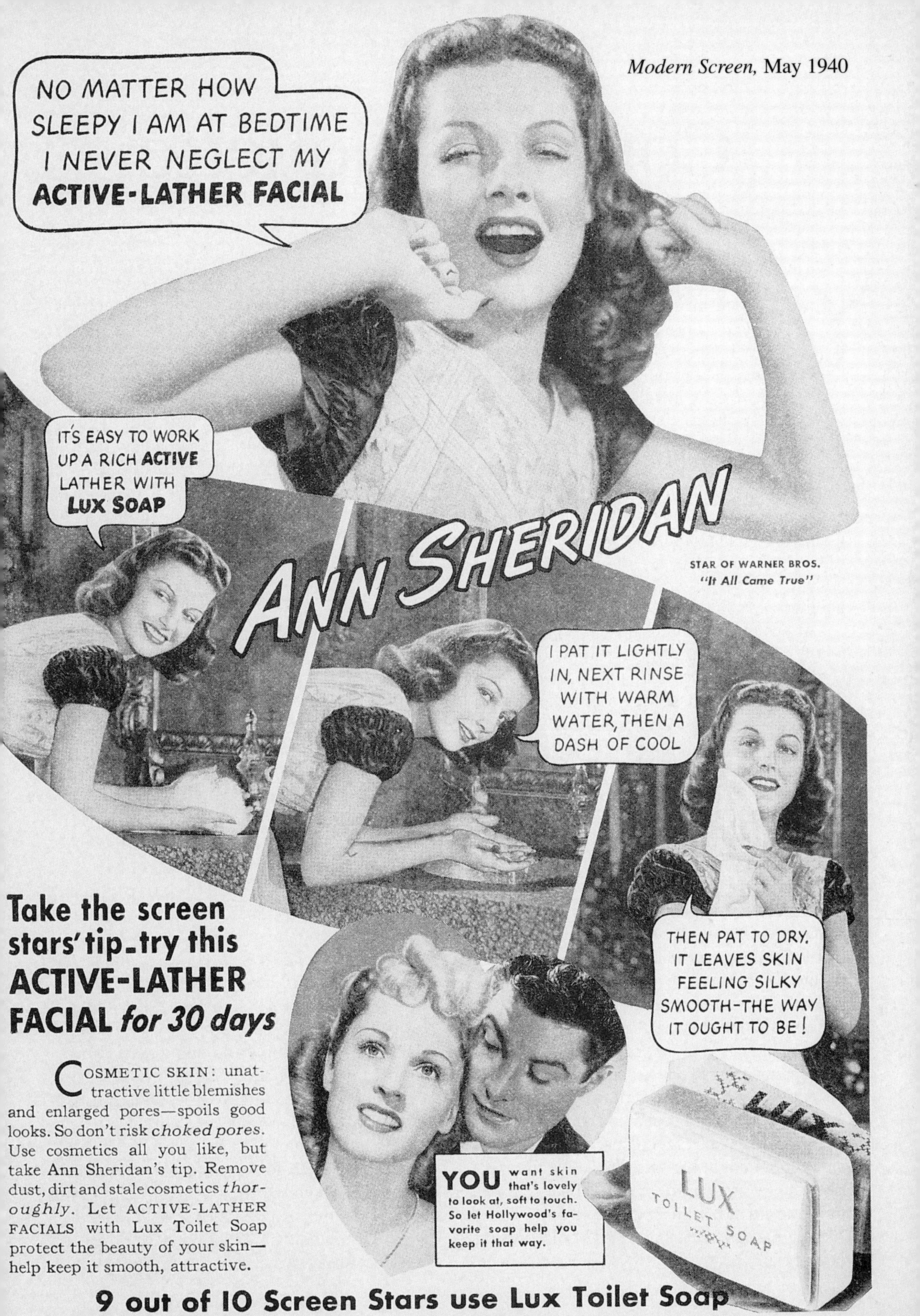

Country Etiquette

By Elaine Carr

Country folks of decades past had their own brand of courtesy, that genteel art of making other people feel at ease. Driving down the highway to our shopping town in the 1940s, I noticed my father slowed the car and did not pass the vehicle ahead. "Why don't you pass, Dad?" I asked.

"Because that's the Wilsons up ahead," he said, "and it would not be nice to go around them."

He knew that, according to mores of the time, going around neighbors would have indicated impatience, and perhaps a desire to be noticed or a feeling of superiority by being in front of a neighbor. My father wanted none of that!

At one of our church suppers, a lady who was a little "slow," not very clean and not much of a cook had brought her none-too-appetizing dish to the table. "Take some of her food, even if you don't eat it," an older lady whispered discreetly to me. "She'll feel bad if nobody takes any." A few others also took generous helpings. Of course I wondered why *I* had to be the one who exercised such etiquette. But even if those helpings went into the garbage, feelings were spared because of old-fashioned country courtesy.

At every gathering, if you look around, you'll notice someone who makes no effort to get acquainted, who stands off silently alone, looking isolated, perhaps even aloof. A lady in our church always had her eyes open for the one too shy to make the effort to be friendly. "I never like to see someone standing alone," I heard her say once. Although it was hard for her to walk up to a stranger and start a conversation, she did it anyway.

It was especially difficult for her to address a man with whom no one else was visiting, but she graciously welcomed such a gentleman, and either caught her husband's eye to take over the responsibility or guided the fellow to a group to include him.

She had the thoughtfulness of old-fashioned country courtesy.

There was a certain reticence in dress among courteous country people. When a man bought a new suit, he might not wear it to church for a few weeks. He let it hang in the closet until a wedding, a funeral or perhaps a graduation or two had required it.

By then he felt comfortable with the looks of it. He didn't have to feel conspicuous around men who didn't have suits, those whose suits might be old or a little shabby, or those whose Sunday best was new pair of hickory-striped overalls. Courteous country people didn't put on airs, show off, or exhibit the "If you've got it, flaunt it" attitude when they had something new.

In the one-room country school where we carried our lunches in those post-Depression days, a dainty spoiled little girl often had a candy bar, to which she called our attention. It looked *so-o-o-o* very good! I asked Mother if I could have a candy bar to take to school.

"No," she said promptly. "In the first place, it isn't good for you to have a lot of candy. And in the second place, most of the other children can't have candy in their lunches." Courteous country kids were not ostentatious with their food. At picnics, church or school dinners, I observed that country folks always stood back respectfully to let any guests, elderly folks and mothers with small children line up for food first.

When I found myself a young parent in the city during the 1970s, I was shocked at the difference 30 years had made. Older adults almost raced each other to be at the head of the line! The country folks among whom I was brought up would have been aghast at such behavior. And they'd have privately reprimanded a child with such a "me first" attitude.

A traveling couple, perhaps in their 50s, stopped by early for lunch at the small-town restaurant where I was a waitress during high school. As they sat down to study the menu, I noticed something strange about her dress.

Because it was sweltery hot weather, her

dress was sleeveless, just a bit bare and daring for those times, so she had slipped on a light matching jacket to come in to eat.

However, she had hastily put the jacket on wrong side out, and the white shoulder pads stuck out like huge butterfly wings on each side. Back in the kitchen I whispered to the cook, "Should I tell her about her jacket?"

The cook glanced through her window and said instantly, "By all means! If you don't, she'll give her husband *Hail Columbia* for not telling her when she finds out." It took all the courage I had, but the lady thanked me fervently for speaking to her, and quickly turned the jacket right side out. I appreciated the cook's inherent sense of country courtesy, and the couple left me a little tip, which didn't happen often.

Politeness, etiquette, whatever you choose to call it, country folks of 60 years ago knew some things about thoughtfulness, kindliness and just plain good behavior—without the aid of Emily Post! ❖

John Slobodnik

Potions of the Past

By Marie Parker and Helen Ferguson

There were five kids in our family, and I suppose we were a fairly healthy crew. That was fortunate, as the Great Depression was in full swing and there was little money for a doctor—or anything else, for that matter.

Mama relied mostly on home remedies. The doctor was called only after Mama's resources had been exhausted.

For a head cold she boiled up a batch of cut-up onions along with some garlic. When the brew had cooled somewhat (and Mama's idea of cool differed considerably from *our* idea of cool), we leaned forward with a towel draped over the head and were instructed to breathe deeply of the noxious fumes.

We would have preferred not to breathe at all, but our breath could be held only a limited time. When we did start breathing, it was accompanied by many gasps, protests and tears. However, the head did become unstopped, along with all sinus cavities.

After enduring the fumes, we were treated to hot chicken soup, which hastened recovery and was much more pleasant than the breathing treatment.

Sometimes the cold settled in the chest, and this condition called for entirely different measures. A mustard plaster was the cure. This was made by mixing dry mustard and grease, preferably goose. When the concoction was thoroughly mixed into a paste, it was slathered onto a flannel cloth, then slapped onto the chest. Again, our opinion of hot and Mama's differed greatly. We yelled that she was trying to burn our heart out, while she insisted it must be very warm to obtain the full benefit. Goodness, I

In spite of various precautions, we kids fell heir to contagious diseases such as measles and chicken pox.

dream of that particular treatment to this day! But aside from a red chest, there were no complications, and it *did* help the congestion.

For a cut, the trusty can of kerosene was uncorked. It apparently possessed a healing ingredient. The liquid was poured directly on the cut, or a cloth soaked in kerosene was applied, depending on the location. If a cut was not too deep, a wad of cobwebs was placed over it. By the time the cobweb disintegrated, the wound was greatly improved. Our wounds were never sutured—the edges just grew back together, more or less.

In spite of various precautions, we kids fell heir to contagious diseases such as measles and chicken pox. Mama knew that chances were excellent that we would all take the disease from the first victim, and she felt the sooner the whole matter was over with, the better for all concerned. To that end, we were made to sleep together, eat together, even drink from the same glass, leaving nothing to chance. No isolation was permitted.

But there were inherent benefits, as it is true that misery loves company. We were never lonely, and could even play together when we were able to hold our heads up. We compared spots, fever and various symptoms, each striving to outdo the others. It all worked fine, just as she knew it would. The misery was over sooner, the itching, whiny kids were out of the house sooner and Mama was out of the sickroom sooner.

Mama was a firm believer in preventive medicine. Every spring, each child was dosed with a generous helping of sulphur and molasses. Our current state of health had nothing to do with the matter. This was merely to get that sluggish winter blood on the run and off to a good start.

Another preventive measure prevalent at that time was the dreaded asafetida bag. Mama made a small bag and put the fetid herb—and Lord knows what else—in it. We wore it around the neck to ward off flu and other winter ailments. The smell was overpowering, and could have made social outcasts of us—except that our friends smelled the same way.

Occasionally an illness struck that was beyond Mama's power. Only then was Dr. Brown summoned, and when he was called, he came, be it raining, freezing, snowing or dead of night. He was an awe-inspiring figure emerging from his elegant Model-A Ford.

Dr. Brown was so kind and reassuring that we felt better just being in his presence. We ranked him a tad below the angels. He did sort of resemble Moses in a tuxedo, wearing his Prince Albert coat, white shirt and black bow tie.

Sitting beside the patient, he gently inquired of each ache and pain, while emitting soft clucks of sympathy. Between clucks, he murmured, "A-ha, uh-hum," never letting on that he realized that he might be paid with a fowl or a sack of turnips.

Doctors aren't like that anymore. They aren't into clucking, they don't make house calls, and they sure don't want any turnips. When a patient is seen, it is advisable to have an insurance policy handy, or a reasonable facsimile, such as cash.

Nor is their dress formal. Depending on where you live, chances are they will be dressed in casual wear like Western jeans, leather belt and cowboy boots. One can almost visualize them on a horse with saddlebags—full of money. And, whereas that old country doctor treated the body as an entity, there are now specialists for every part from the big toe on up.

We certainly must bow to the superiority of modern medicine. Many dread diseases have been wiped out, and science works all the time for other cures, as well as preventive medicines and vaccines that take the place of home remedies. And for that we can be truly grateful.

Still, there is a part of me that will miss those days of siblings in the sick bed together, Dr. Brown and, of course, Mama and her potions of the past. ❖

Things You Should Know

Editor's Note: *The information in this article was taken from a 1907 promotion booklet titled* The Weld That Held Memorandum Book, *issued by Pittsburgh Steel Co.—K.T.*

When setting hens, it is a good plan to set two or three at a time, and put the broods under the care of one mother, being careful to select the best one. In a short time the others will commence laying again.

•   Clean and put away all tools that are not presently needed. If it pays to clean them when in use, much more will it prove economical to bestow extra care upon them before laying them aside for the winter.

•   The iron should be dressed with some preparation, such as the following: "Rosin and beeswax in the proportion of four of rosin to one of wax melted together. Apply hot."

•   It may also be well to paint the woodwork.

•   Trim your fruit trees so as to give a free, open top, no two limbs touching or crossing each other. Never break off a limb on a valuable tree; always make a smooth cut.

•   It is found by trial that horses watered before being fed grain gained faster than those watered afterward.

•   Peas are rapidly coming into favor as a food for milch cows, especially in the winter production of milk, as they are easily grown and are worth twice and a half their weight in bran.

•   Charcoal is an aid to digestion, and should be given occasionally to fowls and swine. Corn burnt on the cob is the best form in which to give it.

•   If a sprig of parsley dipped in vinegar is eaten after an onion, no unpleasant odor from the breath can be detected.

•   In pickling, alum helps to make the pickles crisp, while horseradish and nasturtium seeds

prevent the vinegar from becoming muddy.

- Stone jars for bread and cake boxes should be scalded twice a week in the summer weather—sunning, if possible, to keep mold from gathering.
- Lamp wicks may be prevented from smoking by soaking them in vinegar and drying thoroughly.
- A cloth wrung out in very hot water and often renewed will remove discoloration from bruises.
- Benzine rubbed on the edges of carpet is a sure preventive of moths.
- All of the combs and hairbrushes should be washed weekly in a quart of warm water in which a teaspoonful of ammonia has been placed. Place only the bristles in this solution as the water will loosen the glue in the back of the brush if it is submerged.
- It is a good plan to keep a small dish of powdered charcoal on one of the upper shelves of the icebox, as it is an excellent absorber of odors.
- Rolls that have become dry may be freshened by dipping them quickly into water and placing them in the oven for two or three minutes until the water has dried. They will taste almost like new rolls.
- To make a cup of coffee almost as nourishing as a meal, stir into it an egg, well beaten. First beat the egg in a cup, add a little cream, then the sugar, and lastly the coffee poured in gradually. When adding the coffee beat constantly with a small eggbeater.
- The immense indirect cost of warfare is illustrated by the fact that the Spanish-American War cost $1,000,000 a day for over a year, although hostilities occupied but three months.
- All watches are compasses. Point the hour hand to the sun and the south is exactly halfway between the hour and the figure XII on the watch.
- The world's greatest timber belt is to be found in the counties of Clatsop, Columbia, Washington, Tillamook, Coos, Douglas and Lane, in Oregon. ❖

It's Who You Owe!

By Juanita Killough Urbach

I married young before I had fully matured and still was inclined to put myself first. We were trying to get established on the farm in 1947 on a very limited income. We had borrowed money to purchase a few head of shorthorn cows, which we milked, and sold the cream for grocery money.

We ran out of hay before the pastures were ready for grazing. A neighbor and fellow church member offered to let us have a stack of hay with the promise to pay later.

A loan from the Farm Security Administration allowed us money to seed a crop, but we had no prospect of raising any cash until after harvest.

About this time, the Spiegel catalog arrived with a new credit plan. For a few dollars down and small monthly payments, one could make purchases.

Easter was coming. I longed for a new dress. And wouldn't you know, I saw just the one I wanted in that catalog! Without much forethought, I quickly made out an order for the dress and a pair of shoes. And not wanting to appear selfish, I ordered a pair of pants and a sports jacket for my husband. I managed to squeeze enough money from grocery shopping for the down payment.

The order arrived a few days before Easter. When I surprised my husband on Easter morning, he didn't reprimand me, but he refused to wear his new clothes.

"Why?" I asked. "Don't you like them?"

"Honey," he said gently, "I like them, but I can't wear new clothes to church for everyone to see when I can't pay for that hay Mr. Wright let us have."

I hadn't thought of that. We were in debt to the bank and the government, but to my husband, owing a neighbor was different.

I wore my new dress that morning, but the happiness I originally felt was missing. The $5 down payment wouldn't have dented the hay debt, but now it was I who felt guilty.

After harvest, when the debt was paid, my spouse proudly wore his new outfit to church. I'll never forget the lesson he taught me: Don't flaunt new clothes when you can't pay your bills. That's why even today I don't carry a credit card when I go shopping. ❖

Proverbs & Superstitions

Chapter Five

I don't know how much country wisdom was involved in some of the old-time proverbs and superstitions, but I do know they generally made us a much more cautious lot.

It was probably a wise thing to be cautious in those days. Folks were much more self-reliant, in both good times and bad. If you climbed too far out on a limb, you might find yourself up the proverbial creek without the proverbial paddle. That might be the kind of thing to engender caution.

One way a lot of us were cautious in the Good Old Days was to make sure we didn't get crossways with some type of bad luck.

Once around Halloween when I was a youngster, I had a nightmare about being caught without a treat in the house. There was a knock at the door. I, knowing that we were in for a good tricking, ran away from the goblins at the door, only to be cut off at the hallway by a black cat crossing my path. Scrambling through the kitchen and out to the breezeway, I ran smack-dab into the mirror Daddy used to shave, shattering it. I jumped up and dashed out the screen door, but my path took me beneath a ladder as I left the scene posthaste.

I awoke in a cold sweat. I figured I had acquired 50 years worth of bad luck—well, at least in my dreams.

I can't say that either Mama or Daddy were superstitious at all. I figured that was because they had made it to that stage of life without angering the imps of fate. Maybe they had just been blindly lucky. Or, perhaps it was because they were old and sage.

All my buddies at school, unlike Mama and Daddy, were the superstitious type. Peer pressure being what it is, I guess it was only natural that I would be turned that way myself.

"Step on a crack and break your mother's back!" Chet yelled as we skipped down the sidewalk in the nearby town one sunny autumn Saturday not long before Halloween. I watched as he deftly maneuvered between the spaces between the sections of concrete.

Being a farm boy and largely unaccustomed to cracks in anything but rocks, I pressed him on his audacious claim. "Where'd ya get that idea?"

"Everybody knows that if ya step on a crack you'll break your mother's back," he retorted with a knowing toss of his head.

I thought back to all the times I had unknowingly stepped on cracks. Did the cracks where the concrete had broken count the same as the regular seams? What about the cracks in the boardwalk leading up to the feed store? Those boards were awfully close together. Did they count the same, too?

I figured I had stepped on cracks hundreds of times, but maybe it counted only when you knew not to step on a crack. To the best of my knowledge, Mama's back had never been broken, but Daddy's back hurt all the time. He said it was from lifting lumber at the mill, but. …

I snapped to attention and stopped in mid-step. I didn't step on another crack that day. To be honest, I still avoid stepping on them today, even though Daddy's been gone a long time now.

After the crack incident, I knew I needed a bit extra good fortune as Halloween neared. I spent my last nickel for a rabbit's foot and coaxed a black cat to follow me home for good luck. That would ward off the Halloween nightmares, and I knew there were no cracks to worry about out on the farm.

—Ken Tate

Old-Time Superstitions

By J.E. Kimlel

What does the word "superstition" mean? It is a bit difficult to define. However, the definitions found in Funk and Wagnall's dictionary are probably satisfactory: "A belief founded on irrational feelings, especially of fear, and marked by credulity," and, "Credulity regarding the occult or supernatural as belief in omens, charms and signs; loosely any unreasoning or unreasonable belief or impression."

I grew up in a rural section of south central Illinois. Many of the early settlers were Germans. Superstitions were a way of life there in the 1910s.

For instance, it was the custom to take a new baby, only a few weeks old, outside during a rain and allow some of the water to fall from the eaves of the house onto its face. I never learned just what that treatment was intended to ward off, but it was considered important by some of the older Germans.

When the child got old enough to start to school, he most likely wore a small bag of asafetida on a string around the neck. This was calculated to ward off many serious diseases. But it didn't even ward off other children, as they were all probably inured to the odor.

Ever since the days of the witchcraft delusion, toads have been said to cause warts, and killing a toad meant that the family cows would give bloody milk.

My father … scoffed at those who thought they had to plant potatoes under certain phases of the moon, but he wouldn't think of weaning a calf unless the zodiac sign was propitious.

My father was a deeply religious person, but he never started a project, no matter how urgent, on a Friday. He wouldn't even drive to the county seat 6 miles away on a Friday except in the direst emergency. He scoffed at those who thought they had to plant potatoes under certain phases of the moon, but he wouldn't think of weaning a calf unless the zodiac sign was propitious.

When we went fishing, we always spat on the bait, which meant that the fish would then bite. And the first fish caught in the spring had to be kept no matter what its size, or you would have bad fishing all summer. Later on, the smaller ones usually were returned to the stream to grow larger.

In the home, the housewife also was wary of signs and omens. When a broom chanced to fall across a doorway, it meant that company was coming. The same was supposed to happen if a knife or other utensil fell from the table when the family was eating—except that in that case, the visitor would stay to eat.

Breaking a mirror meant bad luck for seven years. A baby was never allowed to see itself in a mirror; if it did, the child would certainly grow up to be a moron.

When one's palm itched, that person would soon come into money. If your ears burned, someone was talking about you. White spots on the fingernails represented the number of times that person had lied.

Every youngster, boy and girl, hated freckles. However, there was one sure way to get rid of these blemishes: Get up early on the first day of May, before any other members of the family, go out and find a wheat field, and wash one's face in the dew from the wheat. I tried that twice. I don't remember what happened to the freckles; I think I just forgot about them.

Every schoolboy knew that if he placed a piece of hair from the tail of a horse in water, the hair would turn into a snake. Hadn't we all seen that small parasite of the grasshopper about 6 inches long and shaped like a piece of hair from the tail of a horse, and hadn't we all seen it moving in water like a snake? Some of the boys even testified that they had performed the trick!

We were all taught that eating raw cucumbers would cause chills and fever, and that night air was bad for us. Father used to walk around the house at night in the hottest weather to make sure that we children sleeping upstairs all had our windows properly closed. Carrying garden tools like a hoe or shovel through the house was a bad omen, something to be avoided at all costs. And a dog baying at the moon at a farmhouse where someone was ill could only mean one thing—disaster for that person.

Of course, everyone knew that on Groundhog Day, if the groundhog came out of his burrow and the sun was shining so he could see his shadow, he turned around and went back into his burrow, dooming us to six more weeks of winter weather.

Spilling salt was a bad omen, but tossing some of the spilled salt over the left shoulder could prevent the bad luck. Two persons walking together, on coming to a tree or post, were careful to both pass on the same side of the obstruction to avoid breaking up the friendship. Of two persons wiping their hands on the same towel at the same time 'twas said, "Wash and wipe together, live in peace forever."

Every schoolboy and schoolgirl knew that urinating on a public road caused sties, and that playing with fire would result in wetting the bed that night. It was considered bad luck to sing before breakfast or at the table while eating, and a girl never whistled, there being an old rhyme, "A whistling girl and a crowing hen always come to some bad end."

Finding a pin was good luck if the point was toward you, but bad luck if the head was toward you. In any event, it meant that the finder would soon be making a trip. Returning to the house for some forgotten article was bad luck, but the misfortune could be prevented by sitting down and counting to 10 before leaving the house again. Only infidels hunted or fished on the Sabbath.

As was to be expected on a farm in those days, youngsters occasionally stepped on a rusty nail. This was apt to cause "blood poison," but that could be prevented by tying a piece of salt bacon over the puncture. The surprise is that so many of us survived! Nobody— just nobody—stepped on a new grave; nothing could have been worse.

Older persons avoided rheumatism by carrying a buckeye in a pocket, or by wearing a brass or copper bracelet.

Then there were the tansy beds. Most German families cultivated a tansy bed. While this plant produced a beautiful yellow flower, it was not planted in the front yard or the garden where other flowers were planted, but in some obscure place where it would not be seen readily. Drinking tea made from its leaves was believed to prevent pregnancy. This superstition was so well founded that drug manufacturers prepared pills and other products containing this drug for sale to the general public. But the drug was useless for the purpose.

Old-timers always said that for every fog in January, there would be a frost in May; and that sassafras tea thinned the blood and should not be consumed until late in the spring when thinning of the blood was a good thing. Stopping nosebleeds was simple: Just hold a dime between the upper lip and the upper teeth and the bleeding would soon stop.

Every teen-ager is concerned about whom he or she might marry. The answer could be found by placing a bit of a wedding cake under the pillow at night; the one dreamed of that night was sure to be the one. In the absence of a piece of wedding cake, one could collect small pieces of 10 different kinds of wood and place the pieces under the pillow. The dream then would tell the same story.

Every schoolboy knew that to find a lost article, he had only to spit in the palm of his hand and

When we went fishing, we always spat on the bait, which meant that the fish would then bite. And the first fish caught in the spring had to be kept no matter what its size, or you would have bad fishing all summer.

recite the following: "Spit, spit, spy. Tell me where the ball (or whatever) is and I'll give you a piece of pie." He then struck his forefinger into the small pool of saliva in the palm of the hand, and whichever way the spit squirted, that was the direction in which to look.

Our one-room country schoolhouse stood just across a dirt county road from a railroad right-of-way. Playing ball in the schoolyard, a husky lad could easily loft a ball across the road and into the right-of-way. We had a rule that whenever a fielder had trouble finding a batted ball, he would call out, "Lost ball!" and the runner would stop and wait until the ball was found before proceeding around the bases. The fielder would then start reciting the verse to help him find the ball in the high weeds.

Warts were always a nuisance. They could be removed by having a "gifted" person mumble some magic words while rubbing the wart. Another way was to steal one's mother's wet dishrag, rub the warts with the rag, and then bury the rag where it was not likely to be discovered.

Last but not least were the "dowsers" or "water witches," so-called gifted persons who walked around holding a forked stick over the ground to find a source of water. The fork pointed up until the dowser came to an underground stream of water; then the stick was drawn down like metal to a magnet.

Many otherwise intelligent folks still put their faith in dowsers, even though scientists tell us that the stick is no more influenced by underground water than it is by water in the clouds. When the stick turns down, they say, it does so in response to involuntary movements by the dowser.

My father once paid a dowser $2 (which he could ill afford) to locate a spot for a new well. After walking back and forth, the dowser came to a spot where the twig turned downward. He said, "Dig here. Go 30 feet and you will find an abundance of water."

My father dug 30 feet and then 10 feet more and found only moist earth. He then went to a more convenient spot, dug down 20 feet and got a good well. The dowser had advised against

A baby was never allowed to see itself in a mirror; if it did, the child would certainly grow up to be a moron.

digging at the place where my father struck water.

We like to think that we are the most enlightened nation in the world. It may be that we are, but we are still a nation of superstitious people. This is proved by the many daily newspapers that still publish horoscopes, and by the number of people who still believe in such things as clairvoyance, necromancy, signs and omens. It will probably take many more generations before folks become fully weaned away from such—if ever. ❖

Garlic Tales

By Mike Lipstock

My mother was an immigrant who spoke little English and couldn't read or write at all. But there was a thousand years' worth of folklore crammed into her head. I was growing up in the 1920s and 1930s with a mother who was in a constant struggle with the Jewish "malakamuvis"—the evil eye. No way were her children coming down with childhood illness. Trouble was that her remedies always smelled from garlic.

"Here, gargle with this and swallow it when you are done."

"But Ma," I'd yell, "it's garlic and some other junk. My breath will smell!"

"So what, you have a sore throat, gargle! *He* can't stand the smell either."

Of course the next day the symptoms were gone.

Ever hear of crushed garlic compresses for a little fever? How about poultices of garlic, cloves and pepper for a toothache or runny nose? Other families had the aroma of Lifebuoy soap seeping out of their pores. Not us; we smelled like goulash or pepperoni subs all the time. With each dose of her "antibiotics" she would mutter secret chants to outfox *him*. I can remember how the three of us little kids would listen to the mystical words that came from her mouth.

> *We smelled like goulash or pepperoni subs all the time. With each dose of her "antibiotics" she would mutter secret chants to outfox him.*

Overly superstitious? Na, the whole neighborhood was just like her. My Italian pal Ricci had tea bags loaded with Gorgonzola sewn into his shirts. What a whiff that had! And my Greek friend Steve? He had Bull Durham tobacco bags stashed all over his body. Lucky camphor amulets, he called them. The whole melting pot had their cures before the miracle age of modern medicine.

Can you imagine all those "ripe" kids crammed into a classroom with all these curatives wafting through the air? What a heady smell! It drove our teacher, Miss Harrison, nuts. Tears would well up in her eyes. From the odor, or frustration? I never knew.

"Tell your mothers to stop rubbing you down with garlic. You stink!" She would then rub her dainty nose with a lace handkerchief and shout, "I can't stand the smell! Do you understand?"

Of course Miss Harrison was not an ethnic, and we smelled nothing.

When polio struck, Miss Harrison called a truce with her garlicky kids and just opened the windows a little wider.

My mother was ready to meet the malakamuvis head-on. She hung three bags on a rope around our necks and challenged him. Boy, what smelly stuff! Even I couldn't stand her new secret weapons—three linen bags stuffed with garlic, camphor and who knows what. But she beat him to the draw and none of us came down with the dreaded disease.

Once, only once in her whole life, did her artillery fail her. My brother Harry was stricken with diphtheria and her garlic cure didn't work. But remember, she came from a primitive mountain village in Transylvania and still had a few tricks up her sleeve.

When my brother Harry was gasping for breath she suddenly told us to pray real loud to save David's life.

"Who's David, Ma?" we asked.

"That's David laying in the bed."

"No Ma, that's Harry." We thought she was going nuts.

She grabbed each of us. "That's David, understand?"

In very hushed tones she whispered to us, "We'll fool the malakamuvis; if he thinks it's David he'll leave Harry alone. Speak very loud when I tell you."

We listened as she spoke to the evil one, the angel of death. "Malakamuvis, listen to me. You have the wrong little boy. That's David in the bed. We have no Harry in this house. Go away! Leave David alone! You have made a mistake!"

She motioned to us and we started to shout. "Malakamuvis, it's true! It's true. We have no brother Harry. This is our brother David … David, it's David, malakamuvis!"

As we pleaded for our brother's life, Mama chanted in a combination of Yiddish and the other languages she remembered from her mountain life. She repeated over and over again that the boy in the bed was not Harry, her son. All through the night three frightened souls spent the hours pleading a case of wrong identity to the angel of death.

David lived. That's right, I said David. From that day on the name Harry disappeared forever from our little universe. Superstitious? Why take a chance? Dave is a nice name anyway.

We all grew up, left home and educated ourselves, and Mama more or less stopped practicing medicine. When I was 47 I was struck with a heart attack. I remember her visiting me and the look of relief on the nurse's face when she left.

"What a smell, what is it, garlic?" I, of course, smelled nothing.

When she left the room I put my hand under the pillow. Sure enough, there were three linen bags on a rope, filled with garlic, camphor and some other stuff. ❖

The Snipe Hunt

By George Lamb

Editor's Note: *Perhaps no greater practical joke exists in the realm of folklore than that of the snipe hunt. How many of us went through our young life hearing of the ubiquitous bird— at least in legend—and wondering if we would ever be old enough to go with the big kids on one of their famous hunts. Actually, for those who wonder, the snipe is a long-legged wading bird that haunts swampy areas (a painting of snipe is reproduced on page 154), but it is doubtful that any youngster with a gunny sack ever bagged one.—K.T.*

In 1924, snipe hunts weren't the biggest stories printed on the pages of the nation's newspapers. But maybe they should have been, so that the unwary wouldn't fall prey to invitations to participate in one of these practical jokes.

I was 10 that summer. I had been born in a big city, and even though I was raised in a small river community, I was not an avid outdoorsman. In fact, I wasn't an avid anything.

Looking back, I was just plain lazy—maybe not the laziest 10-year-old ever to hike down the pike, but certainly one of the top 10.

My friend, Bill "Stilts" Witt, once asked me why I spent so much time sitting during the summer. He told me I missed a lot, not doing a lot to keep busy. I guess I figured that if the average boy could be in two places at the same time in summer, both places would be sitting down.

On one of the hotter summer evenings, I was sitting on our front stoop, reading the *Evening Telegraph* newspaper. I had scanned the comics, read my favorite cartoon, *Our Boarding House*, and I had just noticed an advertisement for the current Assembly Park Auditorium show.

The big weeklong event would feature Bohumir Kryl, a world-famous cornetist, and his 50-piece brass band. I was about to talk myself into walking the several blocks east to the park to hear the band. After all, I could *sit* to enjoy the entertainment.

Two of my friends, Stilts and Bob "Hendy" Henderson, stopped by to tell me they were going to the band program. When I found out they intended to walk to the auditorium, I lost interest in going. They merely shook their heads and mentioned once again how lazy I was. I didn't argue.

Then they mentioned another idea they had had the night before. The more they talked, the more excited they became. In fact, they bubbled over with enthusiasm.

Stilts began telling me about a big plan they had worked up. I was all ears; I wanted to share in the excitement.

Stilts announced that they were planning a snipe hunt, and that I was to be included as one of the hunters. Naturally, I almost interrupted to say I wasn't interested in anything that would cause me any stress or strain. (The hot weather and all, you know.)

But the guys started talking all at once, so full of the thrill of the hunt. By keeping my yap shut and listening, I learned about the plan.

Hendy had overheard his dad saying that a big herd of snipe had been sighted along the riverbank near where the railroad bridge crossed the Rock River. His dad said a lot of the older men were planning a snipe hunt for the following weekend.

Of course, my buddies wanted to beat them to the punch and hunt the creatures before they were gone. It seemed that snipe were very scarce in our area; only Dickie Watkins said he actually had seen one. Being so rare, snipe were very valuable creatures.

I also learned that the best time to hunt snipe is at night—and the darker the night, the better—and that snipe are very intelligent; they have to be outsmarted if one has any hope of capturing one.

The idea of a nighttime hunt appealed to me (it was always cooler then). And the distance from our house to the site of the hunt was not so far as to discourage me.

Noting my mounting interest, Stilts announced that he had divided the group into three parties. He and two others were on one team; the twins, Jackie and David, and Hendy were on another; and I was to be a one-man team of my own.

At first I thought Stilts was making fun of my size; after all, my own weight almost equaled the weight of the members of the other two teams. But he told me he had selected a special job for me that he knew I would like. I calmed down while he explained.

Stilts' group of three would act as "noisers." They would sneak around to the rear of the snipe and make all the noise they could, thus causing the snipe to run in the desired direction.

When the snipe were running, the second group of three boys, the "shouters," would be stationed along the snipes' path to keep them on the proper course by yelling and screaming at any that headed off in the wrong directions.

Each of us was given our assignments. I was instructed to secure the biggest sack I could find—preferably a cloth one—and also something to sit on, like a box or small chair, plus a heavy rope or string to securely tie the snipes' legs after capture.

All this noise and heading off by the others would bring the snipe directly to me. I would be positioned at the end of the snipes' path, holding open a large sack to catch the creatures when they came along.

We all continued to talk and lay our plans, and in the process I became more and more intoxicated with the prospects of the adventure. Finally we decided not to put it off any longer; we would stage our hunt that very night.

Each of us was given our assignments. I was instructed to secure the biggest sack I could find—preferably a cloth one—and also something to sit on, like a box or small chair, plus a heavy rope or string to securely tie the snipes' legs after capture.

Stilts said he would bring a pan and a heavy fork to beat. Both Hendy and Dickie said their noisemakers would be their loud voices and old water cans and sticks. The twins began arguing about which could yell louder and ended up staging a preview of their vocal talents right there.

We all decided to meet at my house after dinner, but before it got too dark. Some said they were going to try to keep out of their mothers' way that afternoon so they could rest up for the night's work. I liked that idea and went them one better by announcing that I was going to sleep all afternoon in order to be fresh for the hunt.

The dinner hour passed. Dad was kind enough to tell Mom that I would be in no danger on a snipe hunt, as he knew all about what them. My sister, the ever-vocal Donna, made comments about how silly boys were. She said she'd have nothing to do with any snipe I managed to bring home for a special dinner.

The gang arrived right on time, shortly after I had wrangled one of my mom's double-sized pillowcases. I had to promise not to get it too dirty and not to let my snipe bleed on it. That last thought made her shudder. I also had a fold-up camp stool to sit on while waiting for the snipe.

All in all, the seven of us looked rather formidable as we walked along the streets with all our hunting gear. The other guys seemed unusually lighthearted and happy for such a serious matter, I thought. But I figured they had all been on these hunts before, so they had a better idea about the great fun that was in store for everyone.

We soon arrived near the railroad overpass. I was assigned a position well into a clump of bushes up the bank where the trees were pretty thick. Each of the guys said something to me about the importance of keeping as still as possible, not moving a muscle until the snipe were on their way. And I was cautioned to be constantly ready to open my pillowcase.

The others then marched off into the dense underbrush. Within seconds they were out of my sight. For a little while, I could hear them

crunching through the undergrowth, and I thought I heard the sound of muffled laughter. But I wasn't sure about that, and I didn't give it a second thought.

The first half-hour passed quickly. I hardly moved a muscle; I didn't even dare to breathe too loudly. After awhile, I began to hear the usual night noises of the woods—the scurrying of mice and rabbits, the flap of an owl's wings and the rush of air a flying bat makes.

Far off in the distance, I could hear the sound of an occasional automobile on the state highway. Twice I thought I heard growling off to my left, but nothing came of that.

Time began to pass more slowly and, since I had no watch or other means of gauging the passing time, I just lost track. My limbs began to ache, but I steadfastly sat and listened for the snipes' approach. I figured it would be just my luck to be stretching when the prey was being driven into my area for capture.

Occasionally the thought occurred to me that a prank was being played on me, but I discounted it each time. I was too caught up in the exhilaration of the snipe hunt.

As the night wore on, however, I became a bit more scared about being out in the complete darkness as I was. Not that I was afraid of the dark or anything. It was just that the combination of being tired and hungry and the night noises of the black darkness began to get to me.

As a heavy engine rumbled overhead on the river bridge, pulling what seemed like hundreds of cars, I decided to get up and stretch my stiff limbs. As I stood, the wooden slats of the camp stool folded and caught me in the seat of the pants. This startled me, and I dropped the sack and yelled.

Immediately I heard the crashing of branches and the low rumble of a man's voice as he plowed through the heavy growth surrounding me. A bright beam of light caught me full in the face. I put my hand up to shield my eyes, and then the light dropped to the ground.

I recognized the voice then as being

my dad's. When he called to me, I answered, and in a moment, he was there beside me.

"Are you all right, Son?" he asked.

I told him I was. Then I asked him how he had found me. He replied that he had been searching for me with the big Coleman lantern since just before 10 o'clock. He had heard me yell when the camp stool grabbed my seat.

He shined the light on my face and then on my arms. I had been sitting so still, trying to be quiet, that I had forgotten about the bugs. From the looks of my face and bare arms, you could see right off that mosquitoes and flies never go on hunger strikes. I was a mass of bites and welts.

Dad took the stool and Mom's pillowcase in one hand and my arm in the other. I protested that I had to stay and catch the snipe, but he didn't seem to

think much of the idea. I didn't say a word the whole way home.

I just listened while my dad explained about snipe hunts, and how only the very gullible fall for such nonsense. He told me that he had been on the set-up side of such pranks in his youth, but he had never been thick-headed enough not to catch on when such schemes were presented to him by his boyhood friends.

He also told me that my buddies were probably still laughing in their sleep about how they pulled a fast one on me. I knew then that I was in for an awful razzing the next day.

I panted along about a half-step behind his long stride, huffing and puffing more and more as we got closer to the house. When we finally reached it, Mom was in the kitchen. She grabbed me and hugged me the minute my dad opened the screen door.

Mom had the bitter grease out by then and spread it all over my face and arms. She kept

saying that I looked like a piece of raw meat, and to wait until she got her hands on those "friends" of mine. My dad tried to tell her that everything would be all right.

Pretty soon I was ushered off to bed. I was so tired and the hour was so late that I fell almost immediately into a lazy, dreamless sleep. Not even the vision of a roasted snipe dinner entered my mind.

The next morning, most of the welts had gone down or disappeared so that I looked like my normal, fat self again. At the breakfast table, my dad told me something about not trusting everybody so much in the future, especially when it came to searching for things that didn't exist in the first place.

Mom just sniffed when Dad again reminded me to be prepared to take a real ribbing from the boys, and to have them explain how they got along on their own first snipe hunts.

The guys couldn't wait to see me that morning. They were almost fit to be tied, and they tried not to burst out laughing when they hollered me out into the yard.

I played along with their jokes and laughs. I told them I knew there were no such things as snipes all along, and that I just went for their gag to be friendly. Of course, they didn't believe me.

But we all had a good many laughs about the snipe hunt for days and even weeks. I was the goat of many a jibe and remark until we found another neighborhood boy who had yet to experience his first thrilling snipe hunt. After that, the new kid became the brunt of our gang's humor, with me leading the pack.

Although my first snipe hunt happened almost a half-century ago, it remains a clear and constant reminder of one of the great chapters in my boyhood days. ❖

Signs & Omens

Are you superstitious? Do you think that if you break a mirror, you'll have seven years of bad luck? Or that if you stumble with the right foot you'll have good luck, while stumbling with the left foot means bad luck?

The following old-time superstitions are taken from newspapers of more than 125 years ago:

- A falling picture is a sign of coming death in the home.
- Spilling salt is a sign of a quarrel. To avoid it, throw a pinch over the left shoulder with the right hand.
- Shoes must never be put on a table.
- Shoes must be put on the right foot first for good luck through the day.
- Always get out of bed right foot first. To place the left foot on the floor first is a sure forerunner of an unsuccessful, unpleasant day.
- Walking under a ladder is a sign of coming misfortune.
- If your right ear burns, someone is speaking good of you; if the left ear, someone is speaking evil of you.
- If your right ear tingles, you'll hear good news; if the left ear, bad news.
- Black cats are signs of both good and bad luck. A black cat crossing your path is bad luck; but if it should follow you or enter your premises, it is good luck. But the cat must be completely black.
- Laying new clothes on a bed is bad luck.
- Returning to the house after starting out is a sign of misfortune.
- Rings should never be removed by anyone but the owner.
- When walking with a person whose friendship you wish to retain, never let any object come between you, such as a post, a tree, etc.
- Never accept a gift with a pointed or sharp edge unless you give the giver a penny. To neglect this will surely break your friendship.
- Singing at the table brings bad luck, and is a breach of etiquette.
- Dropping scissors or gloves portends disappointment.
- Never sing before breakfast. "Sing before you eat—you'll cry before you sleep."
- Dropping a knife is a sign of male company coming; a fork, female; dropping a teaspoon is a sign of disappointment.
- Do not sing in bed: "Sing in bed, the devil's o'er your head."
- If you drop your dishcloth, you'll have unexpected guests.

Folklore & Superstitions

By Anne Pierre Spangler

Around the turn of the 20th century, superstitions abounded in much of rural central Pennsylvania where I grew up. Some Pennsylvania Dutch folks still cling to these old beliefs. Here are a few that I remember, passed from generation to generation.

Signs of the Moon and Other Signs

• A dog howling at night is a portent of death.
• A dining fork dropped on the floor foretells the arrival of a female visitor; a knife, the coming of a male.
• Planting parsley in a pot and storing it in the house brings ill luck.
• A visitor should always depart by the same door through which he entered so as not to carry away luck.
• A cat eating grass foretells rain.
• A student having trouble learning a lesson should place the book under his pillow at night; he will be sure to know it in the morning.
• A woolen stocking turned inside out and worn overnight is recommended for an inflamed throat.
• Drinking from a cobalt blue glass cures toothache.
• The hand of a corpse rubbed over the swelling on a neck would cure a goiter.
• When a boy's hair is cut, he should not, under any circumstances, throw it away, for if a bird should build a nest with it, he would be afflicted with headaches.
• A toad hopping into the grave of a reputed witch was proof positive of the charge.
• When a woman walks and kicks up her dress hem with her heels, it is a sign that she will wed a widower.

Remedies and Cures

• Milk stolen from a neighbor's cow— or any other article of stolen food—brings relief when given to a child with whooping cough.
• Rubbing the scalp frequently with the hemisphere of a divided onion cures baldness.
• To prevent toothache, pick the teeth with a nail from a coffin.
• An apple held by a dying person until his death and then eaten by a habitual drunkard cures him of his craving for drink.
• Homesickness can be cured by having the affected person look up the chimney, or by sprinkling salt between the sheet and mattress of the bed in which he sleeps.
• To keep a newly acquired animal from straying, scrape fine shavings from the dining table, put it on bread and feed it to the animal.
• To cure a child's fits, turn his shirt inside out and burn it.

Holiday Customs

• The holidays of these early times also had their superstitions. Christmas, Good Friday, Easter, Ascension Day and Whitsunday were holy days. Christmas, Easter Monday and Whitmonday were followed by days of frolic, pleasure and recreation. They were occasions for shooting matches, military exercises, visiting, hunting and fishing.

• Though the elders ranked Christmas as third among festivals of the church, it was the principal holiday just as today. Homemade fresh sausage, roast maw of pig stuffed with a mix of potatoes, bread, onion and spare ribs, plus apples, nuts and mulled or hard cider were served as traditional foods for good cheer.

• Cookies were cut in the shapes of birds, beasts and fish. On Christmas morning, it was the custom of the children to display them in rows in the windows of the living room. Another goody was molasses candy or "moshey," much like today's taffy. A Christmas present was a *Chrich-kindly,* which is the diminutive in German of Christ Child.

• It was believed that beasts and cattle of the stables conversed with each other in a language that, on Christmas Eve at midnight, could be understood by humans.

• A day or two before the holiday, it was a custom for pupils to surround the schoolmaster and demand gifts.

• A mild Christmas was looked upon as unfavorable.

• The New Year was ushered in by firing old flintlocks and pounding on the anvil at the blacksmith shop.

• The day preceding Good Friday was known as Maundy Thursday or "green Thursday," when everyone tried to obtain from garden or field a bit of green for salad to insure good health for the following year.

• On Ascension Day, no work was done—especially no sewing with a needle.

• The night before Easter, the children placed their hats and caps in corners, under chairs, desks or table as nests for the *Oaster Haas.* Early next day, when they eagerly inspected the nests, they found in each three to six eggs of such colors that hens never laid.

• Shrove Tuesday is the day preceding Ash Wednesday, when Lent begins. On Shrove Tuesday, special cakes called *Fastnacht Kuche* were prepared. These cakes, fried in boiling lard, were eaten with molasses or apple butter. (This is still done today, but the cakes are made like doughnuts.)

• Halloween was sometimes not a very pleasant time for residents in those days. Bands of lawless young rowdies threw showers of shelled corn against windows, tied cabbage heads to doorknobs, unhinged gates, carried away railings, removed stoops and porch furnishings, rang doorbells. A farmer might go out in the morning to find that his four-horse wagon laden with straw or apples was resting nicely balanced on the roof of his barn. On going for a bucket of water, his wife might find the spring filled with turnips. His plow might hang suspended near the top of his largest apple tree.

• Those were the days, and those were the superstitious ways of folklore in the heart of Pennsylvania Dutch country. ❖

Foxfire

Editor's Note: The following story by Pearl McFall was printed over a quarter of a century ago in the June 1975 issue of Good Old Days *magazine.—K.T.*

This is not a ghost story, nor is it intended as such. It is a true incident that happened to members of our family in the 1920s. The strange lights were explained to the children as foxfire.

At that time, there were no mortuaries in small towns or rural areas in South Carolina. When a person died, friends and neighbors performed the sad rites of preparing the body for burial, and two or three people sat with it for the night before burial. An old man lived alone in a little house on the side of a mountain. Neighbors had attended him during his last illness, and two men sat with his body that night.

It was a summer night and the house grew warm inside. After awhile, one of the men suggested, "Let's sit on the porch to get a breath of fresh air."

As they sat talking in low tones, they saw two lights approaching at some distance. At first they thought it was two neighbors with lanterns. Then, as the lights bobbed along, they could make out no figures with them. They grew strangely quiet and watched. Presently, the two lights, unattended, reached the house. One entered the porch where they were sitting, went in the door, traveled around the room where the body lay and went out the open window and joined the other light around the corner of the house.

The two men were frightened speechless and sat waiting for a long time, fearing the lights would come back, but they never did. As the story spread over the countryside in following days, men who were more educated said it was "foxfire."

But what is foxfire?

As they sat talking in low tones, they saw two lights approaching at some distance.

Editor's Note: In answer to the final question about foxfire, Mary Bryan responded in this letter to the editor of the magazine.—K.T.

The last sentence of Pearl McFall's "Foxfire" ends with this question: "But what is foxfire?"

Let me tell you a story:

It was a very dark night in the late 1930s. My mother, four brothers and I were walking down a dirt road north of Linden, Pa. The road passed through a dense woods.

As we were walking along talking, we suddenly saw something glowing on the upper bank of the road ahead of us. We were all very quiet, and then one of the boys said, "What is that thing?"

Mother told us to be quiet and just keep walking.

When we came abreast of it, we stopped and watched. Then my brother Delbert said he was going to find out what it was.

The "thing" was over 6 feet tall and about 2 feet wide. Delbert climbed the bank and walked up toward the object. When he was close to it, he reached out and touched it.

The "thing" was the remains of a tree that had decomposed to the stage known as foxfire. We kids broke off pieces to take home with us. We put it in jars so we could keep it damp and put it in our bedrooms, as we were not allowed to have kerosene lamps. It glowed brightly enough to give us a good light and we used it for some time. One of our neighbors told us he had seen it before.

Today, Mother is gone, as are two of the boys, and I've lived in the West for almost 23 years. I've traveled many thousands of miles through 34 states, as well as Washington, D.C., but never again have I seen a tree at the right stage of decay to witness the ghostly foxfire! ❖

Old Wives' Tales

By Karen Sutherland

"The trouble with most folks isn't so much their ignorance, as knowing so many things that ain't so."
—Paul Dickson

"Feed a cold, starve a fever." Or is it, "Starve a cold, feed a fever"?

"The primary function of carrots is to strengthen our eyesight."

"First babies are always late."

"An apple a day keeps the doctor away."

"All work and no play make Jack a dull boy."

We start learning as babies, but much of what we "know" is passed from one generation to the next. And while this information is passed on as truth, it actually can be far from it.

Many of these bits of information are more commonly known as "old wives' tales." Some old wives' tales have been around at least since the ancient Egyptians in 2000 B.C. (and probably before that). They have been found in almost every culture, in every time. The ancient Greeks, for example, believed in "Moderation in all things." The sayings "Practice makes perfect" and "Variety is the spice of life" can also be attributed to them.

We owe to Confucius (in his *Analects* in 500 B.C.), "Practice what you preach." The English were the first to note that "April showers bring May flowers." The ancient Roman writer Juvenal wrote, "The head of the house is the last to know of its dishonor" (or, "The husband is always the last to know").

....

Following are some of the most common old wives' tales. Do you know the real truth behind them?

1. Carrots help you see in the dark.
2. Touching a frog causes warts.
3. Put butter on a burn.
4. An apple a day keeps the doctor away.
5. Gelatin makes your nails grow.
6. Coffee stunts your growth.
7. Confession is good for the soul.
8. Fish is brain food.
9. Mice love cheese.
10. It's always darkest just before dawn.

Do you know if these old wives' tales have any basis in fact? Perhaps the following will help a little.

1. *True.* Carrots contain beta carotene, a natural source of vitamin A—but so do egg yolks, leafy vegetables, sweet potatoes and certain cereals.

2. *False.* Warts are similar to small skin tumors and are caused by a common virus. At least 75 percent of all people will have them at some time.

3. *False!* It's the worst thing you can do. Butter will hold heat close to the skin. Instead, apply cold water (not ice!) until the burning stops.

4. *Couldn't hurt.* Apples are rich in soluble fiber. Fiber keeps our bowels moving; it can help lower blood cholesterol levels, and may even help keep diabetics on an even keel.

5. *False.* Nails grow best within the environment of a healthy diet, and physicians often use the condition of the nails as an indicator of a person's overall diet.

6. *False.* However, the caffeine in coffee can have many harmful effects, including headaches, heartburn, insomnia and menstrual cramps.

7. *True.* Confession is good psychologically, and will help a person heal. A word of caution here, though: "While confession is doubtless good for the soul, it is not always good for the neck."

8. *True.* Fish are high in protein, low in fat and contain phosphorous—all things needed by the brain. However, fish isn't the only food with these properties.

9. *Well. ...* Mice love anything sweet, but will take cheese.

10. *Perhaps it seems that way,* but according to the weather bureau, it is darkest at about 2 a.m.*